MY FOREST

Full of Life

Hannu Hautala
Lasse Lehtinen
Lassi Rautiainen

EDITA • HELSINKI

PROJECT TEAM

Liisa Mäkijärvi
Chief Executive
The Finnish Forest Foundation

Reivo Järvenpää
Secretary General
Association of Forest Owners of Southern Finland

Pekka Kivelä
Senior Vice President, Group Communications
Metsäliitto Group

Martti Rautiainen
Secretary General
Kuusamo Forest Common

Hannu Virranniemi
Director of Forestry
Pölkky Oy

Jukka-Pekka Pietiäinen
Director
Edita

Mikko Häyrynen
Publishing Manager
Edita

Petteri Kivekäs
AD
Edita

ISBN 951-37-3590-7
© Authors and Edita Publishing 2002
English translation Susan Sinisalo
Published by the Finnish Forest Foundation in
association with Edita Publishing Ltd
Printed by: Edita Prima Ltd
Helsinki 2002

FOREWORD

IN AUTUMN 2000, ON THE INITIATIVE OF A BAND OF broad-minded forest professionals and wood-processors working out in the field, the Finnish Forest Foundation launched a book project entitled "The Finnish forest – full of life". The nature books published in Finland tend to show only virgin wilds, their landscapes, flora and fauna, and the only people consulted on the relationship between forest and society are berry and mushroom pickers.

The purpose of the present book is therefore to document the symbiosis of silviculture, forest use and successful forest industry. We decided it was time to tell in proud and positive tones of the numerous dimensions of the forest management and industry, without glossing over the problems.

The story is one worth telling. Forest, Finland's biggest natural resource, is an innate part of the Finnish identity. The sustainable care and use of the forests is the guiding principle behind a broad network dedicated to the promotion of economic, social and cultural sustainability without which Finland would not be Finland.

In producing this book we wanted to steer the reader's thoughts away from the landscape frozen in time. Work goes on in the forest night and day, summer and winter alike. The natural cycle dictates the time to sow, the time to grow and the time to reap the harvest. Even the seemingly silent wilds are in reality a hive of activity. Forest is born of a seed, grows and withers when the time is ripe. But whether it is cherished or left to its own devices, the northern forests abide by their appointed life-cycle.

The Finnish Forest Foundation has been honoured to engage the services of Lasse Lehtinen, a man renowned for his talent for viewing society from different angles, to write the text and of the distinguished nature photographers Hannu Hautala and Lassi Rautiainen. It wishes to thank its active team of expert assistants: Reivo Järvenpää, Secretary General of the Association of Forest Owners of Southern Finland, Pekka Kivelä, Senior Vice President, Group Communications, of the Metsäliitto Group, Martti Rautiainen, Secretary General of Kuusamo Forest Common, Hannu Virranniemi, Director of Forestry, Pölkky Oy, and Director Jukka-Pekka Pietiäinen, Publishing Manager Mikko Häyrynen and AD Petteri Kivekäs of Edita Oy. Our thanks also go to all the other organisations and people involved in the project.

This book is designed for an international readership and has been published simultaneously in Finnish, Swedish, English and German.

Helsinki, May 2002

Liisa Mäkijärvi
Chief Executive
The Finnish Forest Foundation

OUR FOREST

THIS BOOK IS THE PRODUCT OF A LIBERAL FRAME OF mind.

Hannu Hautala and Lassi Rautiainen have spent their adult years making sure their lenses capture nothing but trees, plants, birds and wild beasts with never a human in sight. For Lasse Lehtinen, the ultimate in wood-processing is achieved when he puts a match to the stove in his smoke sauna filled with wood supplied and chopped by someone else.

Famous nature photographers who have dedicated their lives to immortalising virgin nature were this time challenged to seek signs of human intervention. A writer who can cover a page with script without ever casting his eye upon the wet end of a paper machine was persuaded to put into words the essence of the forest and the versatile economy based on it.

The experience was a revelation. The photographers learnt to see the woods from the trees and the writer the trees from the woods. It was an eye-opening experience for all three to discover just what the forest management and industry mean to Finland.

Between us we have, over the years, published dozens of books. Although this one was a commission, we were given a free hand to picture and write about our forest exactly as we see it at the start of the new millennium. The result is three men's very own vision of the Finnish forests, and a project carried out on their very own terms. For this magnificent opportunity we are deeply indebted to the Finnish Forest Foundation.

Having published this book, we see products of the forest industry wherever we look, whatever the degree of conversion, and yet we never lose sight of their source: the Finnish forest.

Helsinki, summer 2002

Hannu Hautala   *Lasse Lehtinen*   *Lassi Rautiainen*

INDEX

A NATION OF TREE-GROWERS

IT WAS NOT UNTIL THE MID-19TH CENTURY THAT the Finns began to appreciate the economic potential of their forests. It nevertheless remained for a German to point this out to the Imperial Finnish Senate: *"The history of silviculture is proof enough that no nation can, without suffering the consequences, destroy or exhaust its forests more than its climate permits. The cold that is characteristic of Finland demands that an especially close watch be kept on the forests, since they alone make habitation in this country possible, and the cultivation of the land may be enhanced because of them. There are forests everywhere, but in the far north, particularly, and in the deep south, they determine the nature of the climate. If the forests of the far north are appreciably depleted, the climate in Finland, too, will turn chillier and life there become more miserable, and the crops will not greatly flourish there."*

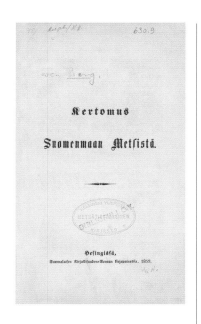

▶ **Unto and Irina Koti-
palo's farm in Kuusamo
has been in the fam-
ily for 250 years and
produces half a million
pine seedlings annually
– enough to plant about
200 hectares.**

The writer was Baron Edmund von Berg, Chief Forester
of the state of Saxony and Principal of the Tharand Forest
Academy, the year 1858. His message is equally relevant
today: Finland relies on its forests for its very subsistence.
The only thing new about this is that nowadays the Finns
are aware of the value of their property, not only to themselves but to the entire continent. The Finnish forests
compose the biggest unbroken green zone in Europe. The
Finns are a nation of tree-growers.

Sometime in the late 1980s my family and I spent a holi-
day in France. On our way home from the Riviera, we
were planning to stop and buy my father-in-law a box of
Pommard as a sixtieth birthday present. South of Dijon
we chose a route through the wine-growing region. We
admired the vineyards, each more impressive than the last,
some the size of a pocket handkerchief, others large estates
clambering row upon row up the hillside as far as the eye
could see. The road signs flashing past read more like a
restaurant wine list than a road map: Nuits St-Georges,
Mersault, Puligny-Montrachet. We found our Pommard in
the cellar of a friendly widow and its strong bouquet would
subsequently become a memorable feature of Christmas
lunch at my in-laws'.

That same autumn my eye was caught by the regular
rows of saplings in a stand by a road in Finland. The little
spruces and pines did not stretch as far as the eye could
see, nor for hundreds of kilometres in the way the French
vineyards did, but the similarity was striking. The forests
are the gardens of Finland! This simple realisation has
since coloured my entire concept of silviculture. And the
more I have learnt about forest economics, the more apt

▶ **Planting seedlings in Kuhmo. Regeneration is the duty of every forest- owner. Seedlings are planted in experimental plots in order to observe their growth and survival in natural conditions.**

find the comparison. Tulip fields in Holland, olive groves in Italy, the rural gardens of southern England in which a retired major tends his roses, or the patch of Finnish forest are in fact just variations on the same theme.

An untended forest has as much charm as an untended garden. It may, as a rarity, have the same momentary appeal that an abandoned graveyard does, but it soon makes one sad. The Finns have only to cross the eastern border into Russia to see what forest left to its own devices looks like. The dreary landscape is a reminder of the state of the national economy. Only an out-and-out eco-nihilist can find lasting pleasure in the devastation inflicted by man on himself.

The solemn assertions made by the European Union on the free movement of labour, goods, capital and services are verified in many small details. The reciprocity between cultures is obvious. While the Italian is building up a nice little business in Finnish mushrooms, the Finn is buying himself a vineyard in France. While German masters are teaching the Finns exquisite carpentry, Finnish loggers are helping to clear up after storms in southern Europe.

Trees also come high on the Finnish gardener's list of priorities. House-builders try to save as many trees as possible. There are thus many lumberjacks in the Greater Helsinki region who make their living from doctoring trees either old or damaged by storms in private gardens. The way they work is astounding to say the least. Not a single flower was squashed in the flowerbeds when a big pine blocking the scenery was finally laid low. One of the men climbed to the top of the tree and sawed his way down,

LR

▲ **Finnish know-how is highly prized in storm-swept France. Kari Rantamaa has spent several years repairing damage in Bordeaux, using Finnish machinery.**

one branch at a time, lowering each log on a rope to his pal on the ground, who in turn gave instructions by radio-telephone. That's one form of gardening.

The Helsinki accountants who suddenly got it into their heads to buy a cognac estate in France were enterprising to say the least. Jostling for a place among the world-famous brands on the Finnish liquor store shelf is one called Le Reviseur. In quality and price this cognac is well on a par with the better-known brands. Of the Finnish-owned vineyards the best-known is Château Carsin, a producer of red and white wines in the Bordeaux region. Master of sixty hectares, the Finnish wine-grower has established a

LR

▲ As in Finland, most of the forests in France are privately owned. This is a European tradition.

► Before the hurricane Jean Balaadere owned 350,000 cubic metres of solid wood. All he has now is the land it once stood on. It will be years before this land is covered by forest once more. The trees have been collected over an area of five square kilometres.

foothold among colleagues who have been plying one of the oldest professions in the world for generations.

Hidden away in Upper Savo, over a hundred kilometres from the nearest airport, is a medium-sized engineering firm producing goods second to none in terms of technology and design. Over thirty years ago a young forest worker from the region, Einari Vidgrén, decided he had had enough of the tools and harvesting methods in use at the time and set about designing and building forest tractor accessories that would make the job of harvesting easier. He has since sold over 2,000 machines to buyers in Finland and the rest of the world, the most distant in South America. At one point Vidgrén sold out to an investment company for a good price, but when the company proved incapable of running it Vidgrén bought it back – for peanuts.

Back in the early 1970s Vidgrén went off to Germany to work in the forests there and earn himself a Mercedes. Ponsse Oy forest machines now have a Mercedes Benz engine and as much computerware as a small aircraft. The founder and developer of "the Mercedes Benz of the Forests," Vielgren says proudly. Today one fifth of cuttings in German forests are done using Vieremä harvesters. So when seven brothers from Heinävesi with not a word of French between them set off for France to help clear up after storms, they were helped by a machine from Savo.

Finland has been growing trees for so long now that it has built up know-how that can be exported to all parts of the world. More than ten per cent of investments in the forest

LR

LR

◄ **Vollrads vineyard in
Rüdesheim. The grape
harvester is reminiscent
of a Finnish timber
harvester. The machine
shakes the grapes off the
vine.**

industry are in planning and design. The world's biggest
consultant, and leader in its field, is the Jaakko Pöyry Group,
which now has branches in over twenty countries. Travel-
lers are thus just as likely to come across a Finnish forester
in the Brazilian rainforests as in the Indonesian jungle.

In Finland forestry, the forest industry and forest
ownership are mostly in private hands. It is therefore
surprising to discover the major role played by the highest government authority, Metsähallitus, the Finnish Forest and Park Service. Of the nine million or so hectares
owned by the state, one third are protected. For histori-

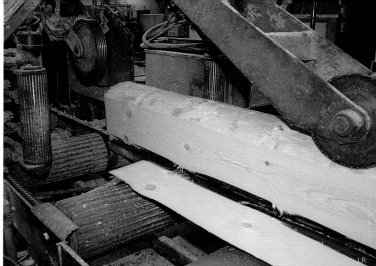

LR   LR

cal reasons the protected forests are mainly in Northern and Eastern Finland.

Since these state forests are commonly owned, they have, with the passing of time, been used for public purposes. In the early 20th century lands were appropriated for the landless population. When young men of marriageable age returned empty-handed from the front at the end of the Second World War, the Government gave them enough land to set up a small farm. This policy had a very steadying influence on society and avoided a great deal of civil unrest.

Where else would the Finnish Army train if not in the state forests? Metsähallitus sees to it that the nature conservation areas on its lands are well tended, that the areas set aside for camping are properly looked after, and that hunting on state lands is not allowed to get out of hand. Since Metsähallitus is nowadays a public corporation, it has established companies to provide special services. One of these is Villi Pohjola/The Wild North, selling adventure tours to private and corporate clients, and another is Laatumaa, a real estate agent.

▲ The Finnish sawmill industry is a major employer in rural areas, providing work where no other branch of industry can operate profitably.

◀ Logs cut into lengths and sorted to the customer's requirements at the Pölkky Oy sawmill in Kuusamo. Processing of the wood close to the source of the raw material reduces the strain on the environment caused by transport.

LR

The bulk of Metsähallitus' annual income of 230 million euros still comes from the sale of wood to pulp, paper and sawmills. Since its lands are in the sparsely-populated regions, in certain localities it is a major employer. Fewer machines, on average, are used on Metsähallitus land than on other logging sites. The highest forest authority also helps preserve the national heritage by restoring former logging camps and forest managers' houses and renovating and renting them out to holidaymakers.

Again, one form of gardening.

Baron von Berg could well have foreseen the future when he decided to end his report to the Senate with these words: *"I do not need to expound further on why it is important that Finland's greatest asset, its forests, be better tended so that the country may, in the European timber trade, reap the benefits for which its space, its wealth of forests and favourable transport routes well equip it. The whole nation will also thank the Government for the measures designed to add to, protect and tend the crown forests, which will in time constitute its primary source of income. The astute officials who today argue in favour of this will go down in history for their contribution to the progress of the homeland."*

◄ **The demanding customer wants only the best, be it a car or a house. Finnish softwood has characteristics that make it in demand the world over. Time to tee off at Strömberg near Frankfurt.**

MY FOREST

MORE THAN A QUARTER OF A CENTURY HAS PASSED since I became a forest-owner. This happened when I bought a farm from an aging spinster. With no one to inherit, the farm would have been left to its own derices. With it came four hectares of forest. At the time I was not particularly interested in the forest, being more attracted to the simple cottage, the storehouse, the old 'smoke' sauna and the virgin shoreline extending for nearly half a kilometre. We Finns do not like to be too near our neighbours, preferring to put as much distance as possible between ourselves and any potential onlooker as we plunge into the lake. "Nature is my dearest sweetheart; it is as if we were secretly betrothed," said a certain Finnish writer a hundred years ago.

Weeks passed before I went on a tour of inspection of my forest. Beside the spring I found traces of a cottage industry I recognised as the brewing of moonshine. Centuries ago it was common to distil spirits in the heart of the forest for personal consumption. Alas no longer. In the 1920s Finland mistakenly took its lead from the United States and introduced prohibition, with the unfortunate consequence that illicit brewing and smuggling took on industrial – and criminal – proportions. Although home distilling is still illegal, it is nowadays the innocent pastime of the occasional urban student and the authorities have better things to do than seek him out. Even the inhabitants of the remotest regions can nowadays order their alcoholic beverages to be delivered, quite lawfully, more or less with the morning paper.

In Finland illicit hooch still goes by the name of 'pontikka' (moonshine), yet few Finns are aware of the word's etymology. By some strange coincidence it has its roots in the cradle of the wine-growing industry, France, and to be more precise the province of Bordeaux. More than a hundred years ago the local landowners up country in Savo would occasionally, in imitation of the example set by their counterparts in Sweden, lay in a stock of wines from France. The empty bottles, bearing labels with such names as 'Pontacq' or 'Pontet-Canet', would then pass into the hands of the farmhands and tenants, who would fill them with spirit of their own distilling. And what more suitable name for this than 'pontikka'? Nowadays a product bearing its own Pontikka label can be bought as a souvenir.

▲ **French wine producers would never have guessed their name would be borrowed by illicit distillers in the Finnish forests.**

Deeper in the forest, on the edge of a marsh, I came across the carcass of an elk. At a guess, it had met its death not from natural causes or as a result of legal hunting. I should perhaps explain that when I bought the farm, it was inaccessible by car, and had no electricity or telephone.

LR

LR

◄ Firewood is a must
for the true Finn. He
has to have several years'
supply in the woodshed,
ready dried and chopped.

29

LR

▶ The *Boletus edulis* is one of the many treasures to be found growing wild in all the forests of southern Finland. It brings a gleam to the eye of Grazia Fancescato, Chairman of the Italian Greens...

HH

It was, and still is, situated deep in the countryside in the middle of nowhere. Poaching is no longer a problem in rural Finland now that sufficient game is to be had legally.

My forest had a few large pines, the odd spruce here and there, a thick birch wood where crops had once been grown, and some stunted pine saplings in the clearings. Despite the fact that I had bought the estate for a very small outlay, I was somewhat taken aback when the harvesting I ordered the following year for silviculture reasons yielded half the sum I had paid for the farm.

HH

◄ ...and is a lucrative new source of income for the "Boletus King" Dalla Valle.

Over the years, my estate has been visited by people from many corners of the earth: from Korea and Cuba, Hungary and Norway, and almost everywhere in between. For decades Finland has boasted of its neutrality and its good relations with both East and West. The guest lists therefore include representatives of both the CIA and the KGB, and our guest book reads like the bookings for a little family hotel in France.

The wife of an American millionaire has produced lasagne to die for in the wood-fired oven of our simple farm kitchen. A British banker bravely defying the midges has, with his own fair hands, picked bilberries from the nearby forest and personally made them into a pie. A musician

from Trinidad sent into ecstasies by high summer and the Midnight Sun once ran amok in the nearby oat field dressed only in his birthday suit. An Italian physician has recited Dante in the original out of the sheer joy of discovering boletus mushrooms in our forest. In a state of euphoria Il Dottore whispered that in Italy there are three things above all others, *calcio, porcino e Ferrari* – football, the cèpe and Ferrari – and in precisely that order.

The question of the cèpe has acquired a surprising Finnish-Italian dimension. Sometime in the 1980s a member of the Italian drugs squad shadowed a Finnish woman as she roamed a forest in North Karelia, espied some cèpes and had a fit. It surely says something for our multicultural continent that this high-up Italian cop is now the uncrowned cèpe king of Finland! A couple of decades on, he annually supplies the most exclusive restaurants in Italy and many other European countries with 500 tonnes of cèpes. The only thing that saddens him is the fact that the Finns do not seem to be sufficiently aware of their national treasure: over ninety per cent of the cèpes are left to rot in the forests.

At all periods in our history the forest has dominated not only our landscape but our mindscape, too. No one has ever found our house the first time without careful instructions. As the roads get narrower and narrower, one visitor after another has given up, thinking they must be on the wrong track, and headed back to ask for directions at a nearby farm or even at the filling station in the village. The forest provides protection in many ways. We have gradually modernised the house so that instead of being a primitive hideaway in the wilds, it is now a house with all

LR

◀ **The traditional joints of this log house are the work of Voitto Holopainen. The average age of the logs is over 160 years.**

► **Logs are dried in the open air in stacks. Traditional log building is an art, from beginning to end.**

▼ **Handling large logs calls for special know-how. The village circular saw comes in very handy in turning them into a house.**

mod cons habitable all year round and connected to the outside world by the Internet and a satellite dish. Yet it is still a place in the wilds in which to seek refuge.

Though fleeting by Mediterranean standards, the Finnish summer is a season of intensive, bursting growth. The early summer sun, hardly setting for weeks on end, inspires the trees and bushes to grow at such a pace that in no time at all our beautiful view of the lake would be completely hidden if we did not take steps to protect it. Our lakeside alder groves and birch meadows are therefore cut back with a heavy hand every other year, and, without making any apparent impact on the landscape we still have

HH

34

HH

enough wood from our own land for the sauna and logs for the fire to see us all through the year. Keeping the scrub in check is like going to the barber; if you do it regularly, you hardly notice it, but if you neglect it, you soon start looking a mess.

A few years ago we decided to build a new house to provide company for the cottage, the storehouse and sauna. To fit in with its surroundings, it had to be built of sturdy logs, something easier said than done. Although Finland is a forest treasure trove and a major power in the log-house industry, buying suitable logs proved surprisingly difficult. The mills do not buy wood past a certain size, nor does the house-building industry need them, since modern saw-mills are designed for medium-sized logs. Timber is sold when it is 60-80 years old and logs of this age did not correspond to our sturdy building material image. But there is no law against thinking big.

At last the message we had been waiting for arrived. "There's a ridge here with a handsome pine stand that must be about two-hundred years old," said the forester's voice down the telephone. "Come and get it quick before some activist sticks a Natura label on it!" A week later the trees were down and the oldest really did have a couple of hundred annual growth rings. The little local sawmill agreed to adjust its blades. The longest logs ran to nine metres. This meant that each log raised the wall on average by over thirty centimetres. We now have a unique log house the wooden surface of which is hidden neither inside nor out. The thick wood in itself is sufficient insulation against both the summer's heat and the winter's cold.

For more than twenty years the last kilometre of the road to the cottage had passed through a gloomy spruce forest untouched by axe or saw for at least a hundred years. It was so dense that there was very little undergrowth and the lower branches had withered away. Every now and then a sunbeam would penetrate the tips and spotlight a deep green bank of moss. It was like a fairytale land in which goblins with hanging moss beards frolicked with the beasts of the forest. When it rained, it rained twice: first between the trees and then from branch to branch and on to the wanderer's head.

Year in, year out, the forest had been left to fend for itself, and we had no intention of interfering. Until one winter's day, things began to happen. Along came a modern harvester and systematically set to work. Within a matter of weeks our fairytale forest had been reduced to an open scrub dotted with tree stumps weeping in the snow, while beside the road were neat piles of logs waiting to be taken to the mill.

Natura, the national protection programme aiming to conserve three per cent of Finnish territory in its virgin state has failed to win the trust of all Finnish land and forest-owners. Many would rather harvest their timber than risk having a protection order placed on part of their forest. Anyone – not just the owner – can propose an area to be protected. The protection decisions made by officials hiding from the owners behind their drawing boards are looked upon as a form of socialism to be fought against with marking hatchets and chainsaws. What started out as a good idea has thus to some extent turned against itself.

HH

HH

◀ **The white-backed woodpecker (*Dendroco-pos leucotos*) is blissfully unaware of the rumpus it has caused in the Finnish forests. Twitchers will race long distances to spot it.**

The white-backed woodpecker, a rare species of bird, has come to symbolise the tug-of-war between conservationists and landowners. Fifty pairs of white-backed woodpeckers are reported as nesting in Finnish forests. No sooner was a white-backed woodpecker spotted in a forest than the owner would rush to sell his timber. In the end, society had to buy the forests around the protected birds. The Finnish taxpayer has so far protected white-backed woodpeckers to the tune of eight million euros or more, which works out at nearly 200,000 euros per woodpecker.

"There are some people in your forest," announced an anxious German visitor one summer's day. That's OK, we informed her. "But it's your forest," she insisted. "What are they doing there?" Whereupon we explained that they were probably picking berries and mushrooms. It was diffi-

cult to make a Central European understand that although the Finns hotly defend their privacy and do not like intrusive neighbours, they will still allow complete strangers to set foot in their forests. What is more, we enlightened her, there is a principle known as "everyman's right".

This right is an ancient Nordic practice going back to the days of slash-and-burn cultivation and communal hunting grounds. Finland has a land area bigger than Britain but a population equal in size only to that of Scotland. Thus we feel there is room for everyone. "But where do you draw the line?" the Germans want to know. "The yard and garden," I reply. "Anyone is entitled to pick the berries and mushrooms growing in my forest, but they can't pick the apples off my trees or dig up my potatoes or pick the strawberries growing in my garden. They can fish in our lake but not from our jetty. That's where we draw the line." The Germans shake their heads. "Don't you mind?" Oh no, we chuckle, and anyway there have been fewer strangers since a bear was sighted in the area.

Many Finns are in fact under the impression that everyman's right is prescribed by law, but it simply means that anything is permissible so long as it is not expressly prohibited by law, or so long as it does not require permission from the authorities or landowner. The right also applies to lakes and rivers. A few points must, however, be borne in mind when exercising this right: it must not harm the land or the forest-owner, it must not, of course, harm nature, and it must not disturb other people.

The provision on privacy in the home supersedes this right. Camping is allowed, but hikers may not pitch their tents in someone's back garden. Persons exercising the right must not leave litter, light a fire in the forest without permission or collect firewood for this purpose. Snow-

LR

◄ **The berry's journey from forest to factory begins with the family. Income from berry and mushroom picking is tax-exempt in Finland. Berry picking is hard work, but a family can, if it puts its mind to it, earn enough in one season to buy a second-hand car.**

43

▶ The most precious of the Finnish berries is the arctic cloudberry (*Rubus chamaemorus*). Its golden berry ripens at the end of July and must be picked immediately. Bilberries (*Vaccinium myrtillus*) grow wild all over Finland, raspberries (*Rubus idaeus*) both wild and cultivated.

44

LR   LR

mobiling always requires permission from the landowner, but rock climbing, for example, is allowed. The bird-lover may not come twitching in our lakeside alders. *"Die Natur ist der sichtbare Geist,"* says our German. Nature is the visible spirit.

Having explained all this, I was quite convinced that everyman's right is simply part of life in Scandinavia and a gift we should cherish with care. We have even wondered whether we should start charging the foreigners who cannot provide a similar privilege except against payment for their use of this right. When the visitors left, they were all wearing T-shirts saying, *"Finnish forests – open daily."*

LR

▲ There are over a thousand bears in the Finnish forests.

▶ Hikers can safely roam through even the densest forests. Finland's national animal keeps its distance from humans and spends the winter asleep beneath the snow.

46

PINK NEWSPRINT

"WHY IS THE FINANCIAL TIMES PRINTED ON PINK paper?"

A good question, and one I have asked myself earlier, but to which I can't remember the answer. We are enjoying the afternoon sunshine on a day in early summer in Green Park in the heart of London and digesting a lunch at a club. The value for money was excellent, not least because my companion paid for it. Over lunch, Tim promised to teach me the rules of cricket. Which he did.

"There are two teams, one in and the other out. Each of the men who is in gets out. When he's out, he comes in and the next man is in until he is out. When they are all out, the side that's out goes in and the side that has been in goes out and tries to get those that are in out. Sometimes someone may still be in and not out. Then when both sides

► **The end of the paper-making process is reached when the end-user receives his quality printing paper.**

have been in and out – including those that are not out – the game is over."

As clear as mud. Like the enigma of the pink newsprint. "It just is," claims Tim, "and always has been." I nevertheless have a sneaking feeling that the pink newsprint comes from Finland and that pink was chosen for reasons of trade policy.

My British friend is a chartered accountant, and inspecting others' accounts has taught him to keep a close eye on his own. He has means of his own, as the saying goes. Or at least he goes in for holidays in exotic countries and vintage Rolls Royce cars. He nevertheless differs favourably from certain other Brits I know in that he has a genuine interest in people and phenomena outside his native isles.

The true English gentleman wants above all to be regarded as an eccentric. To this end, Tim has worked up an interest in Finland in order to regale the chaps at the club. He has actually met Ari Vatanen and it goes without saying that he has taken part in the Finlandia ski race, beaten himself with a birch switch in a murky smoke sauna and plucked bilberries for a pie in a forest alive with mosquitoes. He can take his Koskenkorva neat without so much as a grimace and extol the bouquet of a Finnish sausage with not the flicker of a smile. And he has a never-ending stock of questions to ask about Finland.

"Have we – you know, the British and the Finns – ever been at war with each other? I mean seriously?" Tim has his WWII history at his fingertips. He knows that Finland initially had to defend itself single-handed against

> PRIME MINISTER'S
> PERSONAL TELEGRAM
> SERIAL NO. T 89.
> PRIME MINISTER CHURCHILL TO FIELD MARSHAL MAN
> Personal, Secret and Private.
>
> I am deeply grieved at what I see
> namely that we shall be forced in a few d
> loyalty to our Ally Russia to declare war
> If we do this we shall make war also as
> serves. Surely your troops have advance
> for security during the war and could
> give leave. It is not necessary to
> declaration but simply leave off figh
> military operations, for which the
> every reason and make a de facto ex
> wish I could convince Your Excelle
> to beat the Nazis. I feel far m
> 1917 or 1918. It would be most
> friends of your country in Engl
> herself in the dock with the g
> My recollections of our pleas

▲ **The letter from Winston Churchill to Marshal Mannerheim was possibly the most courteous declaration of war ever to be issued. Finland could not choose its enemy's enemies and accordingly formed an alliance with Germany against the Soviet Union in 1941-44.**

the Soviet Union, thus winning the sympathy of the entire world. "It was the best Finland campaign you've ever done. My late father would second me on that," says Tim.

"My father signed up as a volunteer in 1939 to fight in Finland's Winter War when he read in the paper of a crying need for skiers in the fight against the Soviet Union. There were a couple of hundred of them, all from excellent families, and they received a brief training in Scotland and Chamonix. They were already on board ship steaming away to Finland when they heard on the ship's radio that Finland had made an interim peace with the Soviet Union. It was only then that my father heard that what they needed on the front was not Alpine skiers but people used to skiing long distances."

The British have never forgiven us for going in league with the Germans against the Soviet Union a couple of years later. In doing so, Finland became an enemy of the Western Allies. A nation can't choose its enemies' friends, I point out. Stalin led you all a dance, Churchill included.

"I seem to recall that we actually declared war on you, didn't we?" asks Tim. That is so, I confirm. Churchill declared war on 6 December 1941, but not a single Brit appeared at the front to fight against the Finns. Churchill even sent cigars on the quiet to our Commander-in-Chief, Marshal Mannerheim. So the situation between us was not as serious as it may seem. There is a popular wartime anecdote about a bog-trotter who went and had a shave in his dugout after hearing the declaration of war on the radio. "We're up against gentlemen now," he explained to his astonished brothers-in-arms.

▲ The Imperial War Museum in London.

◄ During the Winter War of 1939-40 Finland fought alone against the Soviet Union. One of the inventions of that war was the "Molotov cocktail" designed to destroy Russian tanks.

53

The situation vis-à-vis the Russians was a completely different kettle of fish. Once again, wood played a major role in the theatre of war. To the Finnish partisans the forest was an easy place to fight in, whereas to the boys from the steppes it was a terrifying arctic wilderness. A myth spread among the Russian troops of Finnish sharpshooters perched at the top of a fir tree and picking off their enemies with deadly precision. The Russians called them 'cuckoos' as harbingers of death.

Communist propaganda warned the Finns against "knocking their brains out on the Karelian pine". The Finns retaliated by inserting birch logs in the caterpillar treads of the Soviet tanks winding their way through the forests when the Finnish mines ran out. Men such as these received medals and home leave. A report that someone had been awarded the "wooden cross" was a grisly way of saying he had been killed in action.

A hundred years ago the Brits were, I enlighten Tim, really and truly intent on attacking the Finns, and with no help from outsiders. During the Crimean War too Russian and British interests clashed where Finland was concerned. This was probably the first time the British had ever heard of Finland. Now before you launch an attack on Finland, I warn Tim, make doubly sure the Finnish ships have already unloaded their cargoes of tar and wood in Britain. In spring 1854, as soon as the sea was free of ice, Admiral Napier was despatched to bombard the coast of Finland. The damage inflicted by his men-of-war was slight, but the cannons stationed along the Gulf of Bothnia burnt the waiting stacks of timber to a cinder.

◄ **The British Navy bombarded the coast of Finland more than 150 years ago, but the damage was slight. Despite the hostilities, Britain remained a considerable buyer of Finnish timber.**

▲ In centuries past tar
was a raw material com-
parable to oil today for
the ships in the British
Navy.

◄ Ships were made of
wood, men of steel. Finn-
ish spruce made the best.
Finnish tourists today
visit Greenwich in Lon-
don to admire the most
famous British sailing
vessel of all time, the
Cutty Sark.

57

LR

"Were there any casualties," asks Tim anxiously. I try my best to recall. Finnish historians do not speak of casualties. Up in Oulu the British set fire to a tar depot. Before that leaflets had been circulated in the town urging the women and children to leave – but the warnings were written in English! The damage was mostly of a material nature, if I remember rightly from my history books. What is more, it later turned out that the British had already paid the Finns for the timber they had burnt to ashes. Finland is not putting in any claims for damages, I add by way of consolation.

The capital of the former empire on which the sun never set inspired us to start comparing historical facts. Wood has, almost without exception, always featured in Anglo-Finnish relations. Ever since the days of Admiral Nelson Finland has supplied the Royal Navy with wood, and especially tar. It seems only fitting to point this out as we sit there in Green Park, for Tim's venerable club is called "The Military and Navy". It occupies the palace occupied by the British Prime Minister Palmerston. It was here that Palmerston died in somewhat suspect circumstances, at his own billiard table. The house has since been sold to an Arab.

"I do know that parts of old London are built on piles made of Siberian larch," says Tim, and they are reputed to last for ever, I add. Tim finds it difficult to believe that my home town, Kuopio, was once a miniature centre of international trade. Then when the Saimaa Canal was opened 150 years ago, this little inland town right in the middle of Finland became a 'maritime' one, a port of call for ships from St. Petersburg, Lübeck and London. On

◄ Forest on its way to the consumer. There is a daily stream of paper from Finland to Britain. On the return leg the purpose-built ro-ro ships carry British goods for the Finnish market.

▼ Modern logistics and speedy delivery are all-important these days. It is only a short journey from the port to the big UK printing houses.

LR

59

LR

► Nokia, the best-known Finnish IT brand even in London, was originally a forest company.

their way to England they carried butter, reels for the thread industry and firewood, returning with grain, sugar and fabrics.

Before the First World War one single Kuopio trading house had no fewer than 28 ships steaming under its flag. In his day the founder was appointed Vice Consul to Portugal, and his son Vice Consul to Great Britain and Ireland. The latter distinguished himself at the beginning of last century by selling Britain matchsticks made in Finland.

The traffic behind us along Piccadilly Lane gets heavier and heavier. The black taxis carry adverts for Nokia mobile phones on their sides. Tim is well acquainted with the history of Nokia and, being well advised of the Finnish companies quoted on the London stock exchange, has not forgotten that Nokia once made Wellington boots and toilet paper, too. In fact, I suspect he has a separate compartment in his portfolio for Finnish companies. I do not, however, venture to question him about this, since discussing money with an English gentleman is 'just not done'. Not only is it rude to raise the subject if he happens to be a man of means; it is even ruder if he happens to be strapped for cash.

Most of the clients of the London stock exchange are unaware that they are buying and selling Finnish industry. There is really no need for them to know. The big institutional investors such as Flemings, Scottish Widows, Fidelity and Deutsche Bank keep an impartial check on companies' indicators and their clients rely on the expertise of the professional analysts.

LR

LR

▲ **Pink newsprint being transformed into pages of the Financial Times at the Westferry Printing Works in London.**

Tim could be from another world. For him, Finland is a hobby. Three of the twelve biggest forest industry companies in the world are Finnish. The Finnish Swedish company, Stora Enso is one of the world's largest and has tens of thousands of employees in various parts of the world. "And a head office just over there, in Mayfair," as Tim points out.

The London press magnates have been buying newsprint from Finland ever since the 19th century. In recognition of this, we have awarded them high Finnish decorations. One recipient is Rupert Murdoch. Robert Maxwell was also made a Commander of the Order of the White Rose of Finland before his empire collapsed. "A decoration is an excellent gift for people you can't bribe with money," Tim admits.

LR   LR   LR

"You're in the business of the future," Tim reckons. "And by that I don't mean electronics but the paper industry." I mumble something about paper being invented in China two thousand years ago. It is 130 years since the Finns began making paper, so paper-making can hardly be classified as new business. "China!" cries Tim with glee. "That's the key word. As the standard of living rises, the consumption of paper is bound to grow the world over. The biggest increase will be in the demand for printing and writing paper. The finer the grades people want, the better it will be for Finland."

The very highest degree of conversion would, I chip in, be an international magazine for men featuring Finnish models photographed in Finland and printed on Finnish

LR

LR

▶ The Finnish forest industry supplies goods for conversion. The consumer does not need to know where the paper was made. The Shotton mill of UPM-Kymmene at Chester, UK, uses recycled fibre.

LR

64

art paper. Just as we are really warming to our subject in a flight of unruly fancy, along comes a city gent looking just like a banker with the Financial Times under his arm. In a flash it occurs to me who might know the story of the pink newspaper. I fish for my mobile and stab out a Finnish number as I sit in the sun in Central London.

The dyed-in-the-wool paper merchant knows the story off by heart: "The Financial Times went pink in 1893. The choice of colour proved to be a stroke of genius and the paper has kept it ever since." He also informs us that the Finns are only one of the FT's paper suppliers. Pink newsprint is more expensive than white for the simple reason that the paper machine always has to be carefully washed before it can be used to make white again.

Before we part, Tim asks whether I know what species of wood is used to make a cricket bat. I fall right into the trap and suggest maybe Finnish birch.

"Oh please...not even Finnish wood is suitable for everything. Cricket bats are made of willow, and the best willow grows in Africa."

WOOD, CHARCOAL AND FIRE

WHEN THE WIND WAS IN THE RIGHT DIRECTION, WE sharp-nosed little boys would be alerted even before the alarm went off. A sickly, pungent smell that would drift with the wind on a hot summer's day from a source many kilometres away. Our first thought might be that the road-menders were back in town, or that someone was having a bonfire, or that the man next door was heating his sauna. But the dark grey column of smoke on the horizon would soon herald the thrill of that most splendid of spectacles: a forest fire!

When I was a child, we lived over the fire station, so fires were an everyday routine occurrence for us. Our dads made a living from them, or rather from putting them out.

LR

▲ **Forest fires started by lightning are nature's way of regenerating.**

▶ **Forest fires are an economic blow to both the owner and the national economy.**

Had it not been for those helmeted heroes in their navy uniforms, the red fire engines and coiled hoses, the ladders, buckets and axes, we children might have gone hungry and our little town have burnt to a cinder long ago.

Every day, or so it seemed to us, a little fire would flicker into life somewhere. At that time houses in Finland were still heated with wood. Firewood was tossed into stoves or boiler rooms, and a spark had only to escape onto the rug or curtains and the flames would soon be licking the wallpaper. One of the advantages of living in a small town was that help usually arrived on the scene in time. Casualties were rare, unless some lush fell asleep with a cigarette in his hand and the ash then mingled with his own.

Sometimes a pan of fat would flare in a home or restaurant, or the flames would gain the upper hand at the smithy, or a spark from the grinding machine would set light to the carpenter's workshop. The sawmills and paper mills were particularly prone to combustion when business was slack and prices were in decline.

False alarms were far from rare. Our dads would only sigh with relief, but our faces would fall if the engine came dawdling straight back just moments after it had gone rushing out with sirens blaring. There must surely be a budding pyromaniac in little boys the world over.

Now a forest fire – one we could smell kilometres away – was never a false alarm. Off we'd go on our bicycles, trying to keep up with the engine, first to the outskirts of town, then into the forest along a sandy track to where the smoke was thickest. The further we went, the more it made our throats sting and our eyes water. We did not dare go near the engines; our dads would never have allowed it

HH

► **The forest fire at Tam-mela in summer 1997 burnt 160 hectares. For a while the land looked desolate, but nature, with a helping hand from man, will soon cover over the traces. The new forest literally rises out of the ashes.**

and we'd only have been sent straight home. The thing to do was to find a vantage point upwind, preferably on top of a hill so that we could watch the fire advancing.

It never so much as occurred to us that there might be any danger, either to ourselves or to our fathers, let alone the goodly townsfolk. There was forest on all sides, and lots of it at that. Had we been asked, we'd have said there was enough to burn. Forest did not really belong to any-one, and if it did, then the owner must be someone rich or a big firm. So if it burnt, no one would really suffer. Such was our logic.

The firemen, too, seemed to look upon forest fires in the same way as they did upon the forces of nature. It was foolish to take risks. Sometimes they would call in the army to dig firebreaks or to douse the ground. Then again, they would sometimes clear a corridor to stop the fire from advancing. At all costs it had to be prevented from spreading to the town, and anyone in danger had to be rescued. Otherwise the rule of thumb seemed to be: let it burn, if burn it will.

When foreign guests here tell me about forest fires that have raged in different parts of the world, sometimes devouring hundreds upon thousands of hectares, or about the fire storms round the Mediterranean in which people are killed and whole suburbs may be razed to the ground, it seems silly to recall my own idyllic forest fires.

I remember one occasion when a forest fire spread to the refuse tip on the edge of town. We gazed in fascination as rats as long as your arm catapulted out of the murky waste, their coats aflame, onto the parched grass. The fire-men would aim at the burning missiles with their hoses before the rats could spread the fire to an even wider area.

HH

HH

▲ Each type of forest
has its own bird pop-
ulation. The redstart
(*Phoenicurus phoenicu-
rus*) makes a beeline for
forest fire areas. By the
time the trees are green
again, the male redstart
will be trilling his love
songs elsewhere.

▶ Marsh tea (*Ledum
palustre*), the rhododen-
dron of the north, is one
of the commonest plants
after a forest fire.

► It all began with a spark. Two flints were rubbed together and the spark set fire to the dry tinder inside a whorl of birchbark.

LR

As the old coal- and wood-fuelled steam engines gave way to diesel, forest fires became less common. For the cause had often been a spark from the engine's funnel. Enlightenment has, with the passing of generations, taught wanderers in the wilds to make their fires in safe places and to extinguish them properly when they leave. The Finns take a serious attitude to fire. Not even lightning seems to ignite our forests any longer, for the Chief Forester almost always sends along His own fire brigade in the form of a heavy downpour.

► For centuries the Finns have had to know how to make a fire in the forest. Even in winter the forest provides protection for anyone versed in the art of burning wood correctly. The night can be spent quite safely in a shelter of branches by the glow of a slow-burning log.

Man tamed fire as his servant a million years ago, but it still has certain mysterious, unpredictable traits that leave us wondering from the moment the kindling catches in the living room fire, relaying it to a second and third log until the room is filled with warmth. I like to point out to my visitors that the Finns feel in very close communion

LR

▲ Today traditional tar burning is a tourist attraction. The bottom of the tar pit is lined with birchbark. The wood is chopped into sticks and stacked in a circle leaning towards the centre of the pit.

with their forefathers as they gaze into the flames of a campfire deep in the wilds of Lapland, surrounded on all sides by virgin snow. They are just as enraptured by fire during the Bacchanalian carousing at Midsummer, when families, villages and societies compete to see who can produce the most spectacular Midsummer bonfire.

People in the northern hemisphere, particularly, are aware of their reason to be grateful for fire. Let me tell you why. The nearer you go to the Arctic Circle, the more important the link between wood and fire. That which we now regard as a form of relaxation and tradition was once vital for existence. Houses were built and heated with trees from the forests and land was cleared for crops by burning off the trees and shrubs; wood and fire formed a life-sustaining chain. "Fire is the fruit of winter," is a old Finnish saying.

LR

LR

In some parts of Finland tar and charcoal pits are still built in the ancient fashion to entertain the tourists. For a couple of centuries tar burning was the most profitable way of processing (converting, as we would say today) wood. The latest thing in Finnish wood technology is to "bake" wood at a high temperature to place it on a par with the best precious woods in the world in terms of colour and strength. As a child I found it difficult to understand how charcoal could possibly burn, seeing that it was wood that had already been burnt!

Another thing I found difficult to grasp was that firewood grey with age would catch better than that from a tree that had only just been felled. Old men would sometimes be likened to "tar stumps", but not until I had done natural science at high school did I really

▲ The pit is covered with turf. The fire burns evenly round the pit and the turf prevents the flames from escaping. The tar released by the heat is run off into barrels. A small pit will burn for several days, a large one for as long as two weeks.

77

► **The Finns are used to the cold. In remote regions wood is an alternative or a supplementary source of energy to electricity.**

realise what this meant. Our biology teacher explained that after a forest fire, there are always a few burnt tree stumps left in which the resin has got so hot that it has formed a layer in the part of the tree where the roots branch out to the ground. "That's the sort of tree to look for," she said, "when you want to make a camp fire. Whittle some shavings off a tree like that and your fire will always catch." And it was true. Your axe had be sharp, but you only had to strike the hard, grey stump a couple of times to get splinters and shavings as red as salmon but smelling of tar and turpentine. Summer or winter, in snow or a heat wave, you could always light a fire with tar stump kindling.

The trains began to run on diesel and electricity. Four nuclear power stations were built, alongside coal- and peat-fired ones, and a gas pipe was laid from Russia. Even in the remote regions homes went over to oil or electricity for their heating. In the past few years there have also been experiments with geothermal, wind and solar energy. Especially in country areas, however, it has been the custom in Finland to retain at least some degree of self-sufficiency – just in case. From time immemorial caution has been a virtue in the collective memory.

We call in at the farm next door and are offered a cup of coffee. As a rule, farmhouses still have a wooden stove, either old or new, beside the electric cooker, and occupying pride of place is a wood-fired baking oven. True, it tends to be used these days to make pizza for the kids rather than homemade bread. If pressed, the proud house-owner will also show you his stand-by power plant. When the weather gets very cold, he will boost the

LR

LR

▲ In the Finnish rural regions it is a matter of honour to have at least a year's supply of firewood in the woodshed. Even a small patch of forest will supply this much.

central heating with a boiler that can burn waste wood collected on the farm and ground into chips. This helps keep the oil and electricity bills in check. Here in the dark northern winter a log of birch can produce more heat than a solar panel.

Another of my childhood memories is of the wood-burning 'fuel tanks' fitted to cars during the Second World War. There were still a few on the roads in the early 1950s. But during the 1939-1944 war no fewer than 43,000 vehicles in Finland were converted to run on firewood! During the war against Russia we used an invention based on combustion: the makeshift bomb, otherwise known as the Molotov cocktail, that later became standard guerrilla gear all over the world.

Far away in distant Lapland, in the little borough of Tervola, a power plant of the third millennium has been constructed using the same principle as the wartime cars. A local farmer first hit on the idea during WWII, then again during the oil crisis of the early 1980s, and now, sixty years later, his invention is heating the whole community. This was not the only wartime invention of a man whose son has now put the idea into practice on an industrial scale. For at his commanding officer's request he built an electric power plant running on wood gas for his section of the front – using an old Ford engine and a DC electric motor.

LR

▲ **Lighting the sauna stove with wood from his own forest is almost a sacred ritual for the Finn.**

Wood-processing mills, both large and small, have learnt to make efficient use of everything brought in from the forest: chips, bark, the lot. Even waste process liquor can be burned as energy. The use of waste wood for electricity production is based on a few age-old principles familiar from my schooldays and the new global concern commonly known as the greenhouse effect. In order to grow, trees need sunlight, water and nutrients, and we have plenty of these in Finland. In summer the sun hardly ever sets. "As they grow, trees bind the carbon dioxide in the atmosphere," said our teacher as she drew chemical signs and formulae on the blackboard to be learnt by heart before the next lesson.

81

▶ **There is heat in the forest even under the snow. The more fossil fuels cost, the more economical it is to use the energy inherent in logging waste.**

In the old days we would chuck logs into the stove without giving it a second thought. Only the best was taken from the forest. Pit wood went to the pulp and paper mills, long logs to the house factory and short ones were used as firewood. The branches, thin trunks and big logging waste were left to rot in the forest. This they did as part of the natural cycle. Now all the energy experts are saying that we ought to be burning wood, especially the less valuable wood; that it would be in our own interest. As I sit chatting to our guests from Central Europe snug in my hideaway I throw a few more logs on the fire. A professor is speaking on television, proving to us that in the end it makes no difference whether we burn our wood or leave it to rot in the forest, because the amount of carbon dioxide released will be the same. In other words, it will not mean any more greenhouse gases. We also learn that wood is a form of bioenergy, a renewable natural resource that can be used instead of fossil fuels (oil, natural gas and coal) as a source of energy. "If Finland is to keep to the carbon dioxide emission limits agreed in the Kyoto Protocol, we will have no alternative but to burn biofuels," argues the stern-faced professor. I translate what he said for my guests, and as I do so toss another log on the fire and feel very smug as a benefactor of all mankind.

One of my guests has noticed that all over Finland people are talking about bioenergy. His paper says that 20 per cent of Finland's total energy and 10 per cent of its electricity is already being produced by wood. A 50 megawatt, biothermal plant, the biggest so far, has been built in Turku, where it burns logging waste, branches, tips, shavings, bark, chips and sawdust. There is no shortage of raw material. The rising prices of coal and oil have made the project even more profitable than anticipated.

LR

The megatrend is spawning innovations and applications in other sectors of industry, too. The National Forest Programme aims to increase the use of wood tenfold in the course of the next decade. Harvesters are being developed so that they do not merely fell, debranch and cut. They also collect up the brushwood and logging waste, sow new seeds and harrow the soil. The inventor of this machine informs forest-owners in a magazine that the waste can well be left in the forest to dry: "When the needles fall off, the nutrients in them are left in the soil, as are the potassium and chlorine that are just a nuisance when the waste comes to be burnt."

Bioenergy projects presumably have the blessing of the Almighty, since brother Andreas, a monk at the Orthodox Valamo Monastery, reports in the same magazine that the monastery has switched from oil heating to a system using wood pellets, cutter and other chips, and briquettes of compressed sawdust.

It is thus with a clear conscience that I make my way down to the lake to put a match to the stove that will heat my smoke sauna. For this I use only dry alder logs. The real perfectionists go so far as to debark them, as the logs then deposit less soot on the stones of the stove. My foreign friends are a little hesitant about entering a black, smoke-heated room. "There's a limit...," says one of them. But I assure them that a smoke sauna is an experience in a class all of its own, in the same way as a Cuban cigar, French cognac or Russian caviar. You don't realise the difference until you've tried it.

◄ **The Keminmaan Energia Oy heating plant is fuelled by wood chips. Tree tips, branches, twigs and in fact anything that is no use to industry can be run through a chipper and burnt.**

HH

BLOCKHEADS OR BRIGHT SPARKS?

THERE'S A 'TRUE' STORY GOING ROUND IN FINLAND about a paper-buyer from the Netherlands who flew to Lapland on a clear winter's day with the director of one of the Finnish forest industry companies. The Finnish host was a little worried because his guest was so silent. "Everything OK?" he asked. At which the Dutchman sucked in his breath and pointed at the big white patches in the landscape below him. "Now don't imagine I'm a militant green, but I have to say that those big clear cuttings are really rather a blot on the landscape." The dry reply of the Finnish captain of industry as he glanced out of the window said it all: "Those are the lakes."

Two hundred years ago the Finnish landscape looked very different from what it does today. Slash-and-burn cultivation, tar burning and cattle grazing had destroyed the forests over large areas. The Finns were reminiscent of the tropical nomads who still, to this day, travel from place to place and burn the wood in their forests in the hope of a better life. Zacharias Topelius, a famous Finnish writer, described the region around the town of Mikkeli in 1873 as follows: *"We see a town spreading from the nearby hills down to the vast, treeless plain branded by slashing and burning and furrowed by the plough into fertile farming land. Observe the endless, monotonous plains bounded only by the low ridges there in the distance!"*

This ruinous trend was halted by the Forest Act of 1886. Under this new Act, the forest-owner was indeed permitted to fell the trees on his land, but only in such a way that the forest would regenerate to the same degree. Clear cutting was totally prohibited. Since that moment the Finnish forest-owner has subscribed to a world view akin to that of the grower of grapes in France or tulips in Holland. The land must be fruitful for its owner but must not be impoverished in the process. Had the Act not been passed in 1886, Finland would today have about as many trees as Iceland or Britain. Sheep farming would have taken the place of the forest management Forestry in Finland is the growing of trees on nature's terms.

I can well understand that 'forest', in the sense we Finns understand it, is not a concrete presence in life for many Central Europeans. The only forest industry product used by every citizen of the European Union is toilet paper. A German journalist friend of mine once explained to me quite seriously at a seminar that Germany had decided to base its own paper production on recycled paper and imported pulp, even though Germany has quite enough

LR

LR

▲ **Risto Nikula from Muhos makes tracks with his snowmobile in a young stand ready for its first thinning. After a cold night the tracks will be hard enough to walk on in snowshoes.**

90

forest of its own. "Why don't you Finns do the same?" he asked.

Taking a deep breath, I sought to enlighten him. Finland is the homeland of long, virgin fibre. There is no sense at all in our carting waste paper all the way up here from the densely-populated regions of Europe. What is more, we look after our forests according to the very latest know-how and technology; we have combined intelligence with wood, and the result is by no means a nation of blockheads. We agreed that the next time my colleague visited Finland he would make an excursion deep into the Finnish forests and ask to be shown some of our most modern pulp and paper mills.

The invitation, issued in a spirit of patriotic fervour, proved quite an experience for both of us. To start with, I discovered I was lagging a couple of years behind the latest trends. The sight of a modern lumberjack alone was quite something for both my visitor and me. For the lumberjack of the third millennium looks more like a warrior from a sci-fi film than a heavy labourer. While we can still admire him for his skill and the valuable work he is doing, we no longer need to feel guilty because he is an underpaid member of the proletariat forced to work in arctic conditions. Technology has once again brought equality to the labour force. Even so, forestry is physically still one of the most strenuous jobs in the world.

Protective clothing is nowadays made to suit every type of weather. Frostbite and blisters are a thing of the past. The logger wears special reinforced boots to ensure he does not snip off a toe with an obstinate branch, as he might have done in past. The next-generation clothing

▶ **Wood-processing begins in the forest. The driver of the harvester trims the branches into piles, on top of which he cuts the trunks to a given specification. It is then easy for a tractor to pick up the wood, collect the waste and take it away for chipping.**

is already being designed by industrial design students. The result will be "smart" suits that can, if necessary, raise or lower the temperature of the wearer's body, dry his sweat or give him a freshen-up shower – without him ever having to take his suit off. An integrated watch, thermometer and heart rate monitor worn on the wrist will advise him how to spread his energy over the day, or so we are told.

Whereas fifty years ago the timberjack, dressed in a homespun suit, would wade through the deep forest snow with his horse and only a chunk of bread and dripping in his pocket, he will nowadays go to work on a snowmobile with a heated seat. The music inside his helmet will be interrupted now and then by a comment from the driver of the nearby multipurpose harvester or the lorry approaching the pick-up point. The man – or to my guest's astonishment, the woman – seated in the harvester cabin will be as handy with the controls as a fighter pilot or a racing-driver.

The machine itself looks like either a giant insect or an angular octopus with tentacles. It is crammed with electronics. This, if anything, really impresses my German friend.

No sooner have I told him all about the smart harvesters made in the Finnish heartlands – machines that are so good they more or less sell themselves in the coniferous zone of the world – than there's a documentary about them on TV. The more I translate what the programme is saying, the more incredulous my friend becomes. Luckily, since it's on TV, there is a picture to bear the story out.

◄ The forest harvester driver has many skills at his fingertips. Like the market gardener, he goes out with a customer's shopping list and cuts the wood to the required lengths.

▼ Logistics is the order of the day. The expert knows exactly who owns the forest, which trees are to be felled and which to be left.

LR

95

▶ **One harvester can do the work of ten or fifteen loggers. Harvesting is nowadays almost fully mechanised, and as easy in winter as in summer.**

Seven Finnish brothers (no kidding, this is a true story!) set off for France with some state-of-the-art harvesters to help clear up after the recent storms. Trees toppled by a storm are much more difficult to fell than trees that are still standing, so the loggers get paid accordingly. Not one of the brothers could speak anything but Finnish, but that was a problem more for the French than for the Finns. Know-how, like music, is a universal language.

The Finnish sawmill or paper mill is already part of a system that chooses just the right trees in the forest for the purpose and transports each one to a predetermined client. This is not only technology: it is ecology, too. Preci-

LR

LR

▲ **Even difficult terrain is accessible to the timber truck in winter. The frozen earth is as hard as iron.**

sion cutting saves nature, no trees are felled unless they are really needed, and to an increasing extent no trees are felled until their destination is known for sure. The cheapest way to store timber is still on the stump.

More and more Finnish trees follow a precise computer-controlled route from forest to mill. This route is a logistic chain devised by the human mind and executed electronically by machines. "When the Dutch DIY man orders some wood and some pine beading to build a garden shed, he in fact sets a long process in motion," we are informed. His order can be phoned in from any-

LR

where in the world, possibly even to the computer in the harvester.

The one-grip harvester sizes up the tree, takes the necessary measurements and chops it into the exact lengths needed to make up an order. The machine is equipped with a global positioning system (GPS). This means it can determine the position of each individual tree so that when all the trees have been felled, they can be collected in the right order. As the logs are loaded onto tractors

▲ **The timber flow from forest to pulp mill never ceases.**

▶ **In summer this marsh would be impossible to cross even on foot, but in winter the frozen earth will bear a timber truck. The upper photo overleaf was taken in January 2001 and the lower one in June.**

99

► **As in Kajaani wood-processing and towns have often developed hand-in-hand. The 'smoke' rising from the paper mill is pure steam, and even the towns are like gardens in their summer greenery.**

known as forwarders, they are weighed. While the forwarders transport the logs to the roadside, timber trucks equipped with satellite positioners and digital maps may be taking the optimal route to the pick-up point. Each wood grade can then be delivered to the client by the shortest possible route.

Growing and felled trees are measured with a palmtop computer. The thickness, weight and volume can be determined to within a few centimetres from hundreds of metres away with a laser calculator. All the data and information is then fed straight back to the client's data network so that he in turn can proceed with his planning.

We were given to believe that, in the future, only robots will work in the forests. Walking machines, flying chainsaws and automatic collectors will be hard at work round-the-clock and controlled by an operator at a city computer.

The Finnish forest machine and timber truck contractors are self-employed entrepreneurs, though their machines and trucks may often bear the name of the company to which they are contracted large. Contracts such as these are made to the value of € 700 million a year, and there are contractors all over the country. Thus once again forest enterprise provides the potential for a good life and standard of living in even the remotest region.

The preacher delivering this technological sermon suddenly breaks off to tell us that in some places you can order a man with a horse to do your felling. He will then deliver the logs to the roadside, one load at a time, without breaking a single branch unnecessarily. To say nothing of the urban tree doctors who leap about city gardens like flying squirrels, lopping off branches one at a time to give the roses more light.

LR

"But what about the logging waste?" my friend wants to know. "What do you do about the environment?" I quickly swallow any scathing remarks I might have made about the way the DDR treated its environment. On German motorways and the quality of the air in the Ruhrgebiet. I may not be an expert, but I do know that more than half the waste paper is collected in Finland and Sweden. The only emissions from a modern pulp mill are the occasional whiff of cabbage. The same volume of wood is nowadays used to make twice as much board and paper as in the 1960s.

Thanks to the technological advances, the forest industry has increased its output many times over yet, at the same time, reduced its emissions into the air and water to a fraction of what they used to be. Finnish wood products already bind more carbon dioxide than the amount emitted by the entire Finnish forest industry. The spent process liquor is burnt as energy. A big pulp mill is also a power plant. Added to which, I say, as I wag my finger, wood is a renewable natural resource! The more we use wood instead of plastic, steel, aluminium or rubber, the less carbon dioxide we will emit into the atmosphere and the better we can slow down the greenhouse effect.

It is a recognised fact that the most rapidly expanding markets of Asia will not require large quantities of expensive quality paper for many years to come. Yet quality is what the Finnish forest industry is aiming at as its key competitive factor. Production is already highly automated, and Finland will never be a country where labour is cheap. In the future savings will have to be sought in materials and their processing.

Some four-hundred biologists, geneticists, botanists and biochemists are putting their heads together in a research project called Wood Wisdom. Just as medicine is developing precision drugs, so Finnish scientists are cultivating precision trees. Drawing on genetic technology, it will in the future be possible to grow the optimal trees for a specific paper grade; their lignin content will be lower, and they will be more resistant to cold and pollution. Lignin makes the wood strong and accounts for 20-30 per cent of the weight of the wood. The pulp and paper industry then tries to get rid of it, and it is the lignin that keeps the mill's environmental engineers busy. Either the lignin content must be reduced, or it must be converted into some more easily extractable form.

And finally a neat piece of information: Did you know that the first section of the tunnel piping drinking water to the City of Helsinki is made of wood? It is 350 metres long and two metres in diameter. Why wood? Because under water wood neither rots nor rusts and readily accommodates itself to the movements of the water. No, I didn't think you would know that!

My German journalist friend left the land of the fir trees with his head spinning. Maybe, like the Dutchman, he gazed down upon the snowy landscape from the aircraft window and tried to guess which of the patches were lakes and which were clear cuts. The only present he had to take home with him was a little bird carved from a single piece of wood, and maybe a growing realisation that far away in the north, people are not only growing and cutting forests down, but also planting intelligence.

◀ Wood-processing industry and traditional farming live side-by-side in complete harmony in Jämsä. Thanks to the strict air pollution regulations, the countryside is clean even close to mills.

WAR OF WORDS
IN THE FOREST

A DARK LADY IN EARLY MIDDLE AGE DRESSED IN A green rain cape stands amid the whispering pines of a Finnish forest giving a talk to a similarly-attired group of men and women. From a distance, they could be straight out of Tolkien: Hobbits straining to catch the story of the "Lord of the Rings". On closer inspection, one might be forgiven for believing them to be adherents of some religious sect gathered in the dripping forest to recite pantheistic chants.

The explanation is, however, far more mundane. And very Finnish. The assembled company are nothing less than politicians, civil servants, businessmen, civil activists and journalists. They have gathered in the forest for what is known as a Forest Academy something which has been held in Finland since the mid-1990s. The idea behind the Academy is to enlighten persons in key positions on for-

▶ **Finnish politicians and people in authority at the Forest Academy have all sorts of questions about forests and are sometimes highly sceptical. One of the students on the course given by Dr Eeva Hellström was Mr Pentti Arajärvi, husband of the Finnish President.**

est issues. They also provide an opportunity for forest-owners and industry to discuss national and international issues with people whom they may not otherwise come in contact with. The principal of the Academy is the dark lady in the green cape, Dr Eeva Hellström.

Is it really necessary to explain forests to people who do not directly make a living from them? I raise this question at the course centre later that evening. It goes without saying that the centre is a forest hideaway far from the city lights – and beside a lake, of course. "Finland lives off its forests," says our lady principal. "The country is so heavily dependent on its forests and its nature for its well-being that the forest industry cannot afford to ignore the social debate. And by the industry I mean the entire forest cluster, the complete chain, from the trees in the forest to the mill and the end-consumer."

The Finnish tendency to seek consensus rather than conflict is another major factor behind these courses. It explains why, gathered round the same table, are people who would probably never meet another in the normal way. Given a different context, the secretary of the Green League would be more likely to face the large forest-owner holding a militant placard, but here they are amicably discussing the principles of ecological and social sustainability. "In a forum like this you are bound to broaden your outlook. It's a positive form of brainwashing for everyone involved. After only a few years, we can already see that things like budget talks with the Government are easier now that top civil servants have been made aware of the long time-scale in our line of business."

▶ **The Forest Academy students in the age-old spruce forest could well have been Hobbits in "The Lord of the Rings".**

Our principal is an expert on forest disputes in various countries. It came as a slight surprise to the people on our course that the biggest disputes worldwide have taken place in Finland and on the northwest coast of the United States. Elsewhere they are virtually unknown, or are certainly not on the same scale. "In my research I looked into experiences in six countries to compare conditions and phenomena in a few countries with lots of forests. Some forty years ago there was occasional criticism of the forest economy in various parts of the world. Disputes were usually local. But as forest resources began to be used more effectively and the standard of living rose, people began to look on the forests as places of recreation as well, and a wave of national forest conflicts swept the Western world. And of course, it's no coincidence, that it was just at this time that the environmental movements were gaining public support."

To exaggerate slightly, we can say that the Finnish forests began to be exploited in a big way in the 1960s and 1970s, and following in the wake of the big new machines came the environmental activists, who began writing about the subject in their own media. Doring the next decade city hikers discovered the Finnish wilds and old forests. Many of them became nature-lovers overnight. Thanks to the universal right of access to Finnish forests, they were now roaming through forests owned by someone else.

Then once the TV cameras finally found their way into the forests and wilds, things began to happen. City-dwellers saw news flashes of hot-headed young activists chained to enormous harvesters while forest-owners conferred with the police at the edge of the clearing. I remember when I did my national service there was one

city guy who found it difficult to accept orders from the officious NCOs. So I was not surprised to see on the TV news and in the papers some years later, the same guy being carried off by the police until he hit on the idea of chaining himself to a tree. He even got into Parliament on the strength of this.

▲ **Forest and nature conflicts are a Finnish speciality. Sometimes the authorities have to step in and arbitrate.**

Who needs research into conflict? Could future wars be averted by analysing those past? "The previous forest conflict study only went as far as the early 1980s, so I

HH

▲ Beauty is in the eye of the beholder. An untended forest may have a certain charm, but it is the result of neglect. Silviculture is horticulture Finnish style. A thinned forest gets light, the trees grow and earn money.

decided to continue it and broaden the perspective to make it as global as possible. The results are probably no use in solving individual disputes, but the mere knowledge that others have problems, too, and that each country solves them in a different way is conducive to mutual understanding. I have reported my research findings to industrial giants, government officials and environmental organisations."

Although Dr Hellström makes her living from the forestry, she has gone the same way as many a researcher before her: she has come to understand both parties to the

▶ **Give and take. The birches protect the spruces from the cold until they are big enough to manage alone. Then it will be the birches' turn to go.**

dispute. "From industry's point of view, environmental conflicts have, of course, been a threat. Only recently have people begun to realise that they may also be a strength. The forest management needs to be viewed more widely. It's not just timber production. For the Finns, the forests are a natural resource, endowed not only with economic values but with ecological, social and cultural values as well. Conflicts help us identify topical problems and keep the authorities on their toes."

Dr Hellström grew up in a little town in Central Finland. Her father has always owned forest, so she has had a feel for the forests ever since childhood. "I wanted to study landscape architecture, but I didn't get in, so I moved over to forest management instead. I've agreed with my father that I'll gradually take over the practical management of his forests, the timber selling and things like that."

Why is it that the Finns speak of "forest wars" while the Swedes prefer to talk about "forest disputes" and the Germans "forest debates"? Dr Hellström feels that all societies have their own, time-honoured way of handling disagreements. Their tolerance of conflicts also differs. "Things that may, in one culture, seem like a friendly chat may in another be classed as a violent dispute, and vice versa."

Since it has been impressed upon us that we must ask questions and be active pupils, I ask Dr Hellström what she found most surprising in the foreign countries she studied. She pauses before saying that cultural differences are always what, at the end of the day, astonish her most. "In the southern US states it was the accepted thing for the

HH

▶ **Beard lichens and mosses are a sign that the forest is not suffering from air pollution.**

LR

undergrowth to be bulldozed after harvesting so that only the soil was left. This was really drastic by Nordic standards. In the UK there's no land register in which you can check who owns a particular plot of forest. In France the general public couldn't care less about protected forests. And in Norway there are virtually no arguments on such issues." Eeva Hellström stops to think before continuing: "The thing I remember possibly best of all was the American rattle-snake I stood on for a long time without realising it!"

The ancient Finnish forest brings us back to earth again. Here we were, members of a new economy and information society with nothing else to think about except trends and brands, bonds and options, standing at the foot of an

LR

◄ **Fungi growing on a rotting tree are an indication that the features of an old forest have been preserved.**

ancient fir tree listening to someone describing the importance of long-fibred raw wood to the global paper industry. Here we were, assured only two decades ago that the whole world would soon be one paper-free office, being told that the consumption of paper in offices is steadily growing. Here we were, led by the experts to believe that in the third millennium newspapers would no longer exist in the traditional sense of the word and that books would be read on screen, being told that newspapers and books are selling better than ever and that in the printing houses the demand for paper is steadily growing.

"A virtual economy needs a real economy to fall back on," said the Minister in his opening speech to the seminar. "Instead of two feet, Finnish exports are now standing on three: forest, metal and information technology." He urged us to follow what happens when IT meets for-

◄ Regeneration is not always a beautiful sight. The forest, like a garden, needs weeding and hoeing. This machine causes the seeds to fall automatically as it tills the soil.

est industry products. "The technology already exists for processors to print on paper. Messages can be added to packing board. Milk cartons can be made to "complain" if kept in the fridge for too long. "Smart" paper and packs are the offspring of an alliance between old and new technology." At this point in the Minister's speech I find myself recalling our principal telling us that the fir tree we are standing under is two hundred years old.

It is only on a course like this that the urban paper consumer gains any sort of insight into what the use of the forests truly means. The end product is made and marketed by a supranational listed giant, but at the other end of the chain are the individual forest-owners, the tree-growers whose attitude to their property is highly emotional. Every new regulation is another intrusion. The forest-owner who earns his or her living from growing and selling wood and who is part of a long line of forest-owners is more sceptical towards regulation than the city-dweller who has inherited a little clump of trees.

The more city-owners there are who leave their forests untouched, the more problems industry will have in obtaining an adequate supply of wood. Unless a forest has something unique to offer, protection is like leaving a garden untended. Failure to tend it does not protect it. Money rots in the forest. As Finnish society becomes more and more urban, the forest management is increasingly having to enlighten the city forest-owner. Industry will not get its wood unless it is worth someone growing it. Forest inheritancies should be treated in the same way as

LR

◀ **Rafsec Oy, a subsidiary of UPM-Kymmene, makes smart labels that will at some point replace barcodes on parcels, air baggage and individual consumer goods. They add a memory to products and goods.**

a dispersed portfolio. There may be many types of forest in as little as ten hectares.

Our course also taught us that forest-related tourism is still economically insignificant but growing all the time. Nature and adventure tours are becoming increasingly popular from year to year. Once tours are organised in such a way that they acquire economic significance, the problems begin. Snowmobiles, dog teams and horse-riding do not suit protected areas. They are acceptable in ordinary forests, but until the forest-owner can expect to earn more from tourism than from the sale of wood, the conflicts will continue.

It is still, however the conflicts between forest-owners and conservationists that are the most difficult to handle. There was one forest-owner on the course who felt the protection of the white-backed woodpecker had run out of all proportion. "Birds may have small brains, but they are still capable of finding a new tree to nest in if I happen to chop the old one down," he said.

Dr Hellström recalls a similar dispute the other side of the world. "Conservationists on the northwest coast of the United States had the northern spotted owl proclaimed an endangered species in the early 1990s. The courts then prohibited felling in the bulk of the state's forests. Although the forests there were state-owned, the ban had such an impact on employment in the region that the Government was forced to lift it, and even environmental legislation was somewhat watered down. I only hope that in Finland we can settle similar disputes more constructively."

Central Europeans sometimes delude themselves that clear cutting in the northern regions may cause irreversible destruction; that the last of the natural forests will be chopped down and the environment will go by the board. This Central European attitude is not, however, compatible as such with the very different northern forest zone. The forests of Central and Western Europe have not been natural forests for centuries; their trees are all cultivated or planted. The Netherlands have no original forests. By contrast, only a quarter of the trees in the Finnish and Swedish forests are sown or planted; the rest are the result of natural regeneration. And considering the total area covered by forest, that is a lot of trees. In the cold, barren regions of Northern Finland nature regeneration is helped by planting trees.

The Finnish forest management has set itself the ambitious goal of incorporating every possible interest within one vast forest cluster: wood production, forest tree breeding, recreation and environmental protection.

The principle is concord, not conflict. "We have reached the point where environmental lobbies can give the industry their ecological know-how and in return we can give them the latest knowledge on the use of wood as an ecological, renewable material," are Dr Hellström's concluding words.

OWNERS IN TOWN
AND COUNTRY

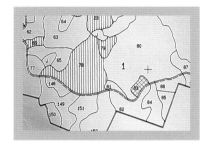

ONE FINN IN FIVE OWNS AT LEAST SOME FOREST. In other words, Finland has a million small forest-owners, from nearly 400,000 families. The number of Finns who earn their living entirely from forest ownership also runs into thousands.

I turn off the motorway onto a surfaced main road and drive straight for 50 kilometres until I reach a dirt track that twists and turns through rich forest landscape that would be any rally designer's dream. I'm more than two hours out of Helsinki before I recognise the long lake mentioned in my driving instructions, and I still have several kilometres to go along the lake. Suddenly I catch sight of a house that fits the description I have been given.

LR

LR

◀ A relascope is an important tool for the forest-owner, who uses it to determine the volume of wood per hectare.

Eine Rosenberg-Riihimäki rushes out to welcome me. A farmer's daughter, she became a full-time forest-owner when Finland joined the European Union. The reason was simple: once Finland became a Member State, growing cereals ceased to be profitable but forest ownership did not. A slim, dark woman in her fifties, she is clearly in the right job, at one with her forest. In other words, she cares about her trees, something you notice at once.

To give me a graphic picture of the entire 600 hectares we spread the map attached to the estate's forest plan on the parlour table's lace cloth. Plans such as this are made for ten years at a time. This one consists of a pile of maps and documents kept in a thick box file and shows the estimated condition of the forest more or less trunk by trunk.

◀ Eine Rosenberg-Riihimäki is a full-time forest-owner. For her work and leisure are one and the same thing.

129

▶ **The annual growth of a spruce tip (*Picea abies*) looks like this.**

LR

The file will soon be transferred to CD-ROM so that it can be read on screen and sent in digital format.

Do you know every tree in your forest?
She laughs at my question, but glancing at the map admits that she can indeed recall the species and stage of growth of each lot in the estate. "I have to keep my eye on things all the time!" she points out. "In summer I go out and take a look at what's happening at least once a week." And in winter? "In winter it's enough if I inspect any cuttings which may be going on."

Some of Eine Rosenberg's forests were inherited from her father, and some she has purchased since. She lives in the old family home and is completely dedicated to tending her forests. Her husband is a genuine farmer with a

▶ **A pine (*Pinus sylvestris*) grows about 20 centimetres a year.**

LR

▶ **Tending a seedling stand with a clearing saw is a job for a professional lumberjack. Paavo Pentikäinen from Hartola is just the man for the job.**

LR

LR

LR

132

► **Young, fairly thin heath forest is a berry-picker's dream. Bilberries, especially, thrive in well-tended forest.**

farm of his own at Orimattila, an hour-and-a-half's drive away. The division of labour seems to work well. Mrs Rosenberg also takes a broader interest in silviculture. She is chairman of – and the only woman on – the board of the forest management association for the region. These local associations are a very Finnish institution allowing private forest-owners to tend their forests by mutual agreement. Foreigners come all the way to Finland just to learn about them.

"The forest management association is an economical way of managing your property, especially for urban forest-owners. If only more townsfolk would take a more active role in them," she says. Why? "Although, in principle, townsfolk are just as enthusiastic as country folk, I'm afraid some forests may not get all the attention they deserve simply because their owners don't know what to do. Sometimes, if several people have inherited a forest estate, nothing gets done while they argue about who owns what."

Some people are worried that as more and more people inherit forest land, ownership will become increasingly fragmented and pass into the hands of a growing number of townspeople. The problem here is that a second or third-generation owner living in the city who does not rely on the forests for his livelihood may fail to look after his property. Only the essential forestry measures will be carried out, and nothing more. The city owner whose environmental conscience has been pricked may also seek a preservation order on forests where the biodiversity is of little significance but that would, if protected, be an out-and-out impediment to the forest management.

LR

Listening to my hostess speak, it really sounds as if her heart is in her forests. She wants to live with them. "I also have to go and see whether nature has upset the plans we humans have made. The sapling stands are a constant worry. Round here ordinary grass tends to choke the saplings before they've had a chance to get established. Or they may be chewed off by elks, or copses may spring up and shut out the light."

Forest ownership is a long-term commitment. In a country like Finland, the natural life span of one generation of trees can be anything from sixty to a hundred years. "In twenty years you may have had two sapling stands in an old forest." Owners here can expect to have wood to sell thirty years after planting. "The financial result of the first harvest, carried out manually, is just about zero, but if it can be done mechanically you may have something small to show for it."

The first few years after establishing a sapling stand call for a lot of work and supervision. Then for a while the owner can trust the forces of nature. The summer after a regeneration felling the land has to be tilled with a harrow or screefed with an excavator. New saplings can then be planted or seeds sown the summer after that. In certain types of forests some trees are left standing and these seed trees, as they are called, do the job without any human assistance. The third year is spent watching the saplings grow and cutting back the undergrowth threatening to choke them. In southern Finland, where the soil is luxuriant, it may be necessary to continue cutting back for years before the trunks reach a safe height.

▲ The certificate issued by an impartial body is proof that the estate forests are part of the European forest stewardship system.

◀ After the Second World War Finns returning from the front or evacuated from the part of the country ceded to Russia were given land to farm. In the arctic conditions farming did not always provide a sufficient income, but a few hectares of forest would help a family to survive.

LR

▲ **Selling timber is always exciting. The price depends on supply and demand.**

On an estate of six hundred hectares there is always some timber ready to sell. Eine Rosenberg sells something every year to keep the areas for regeneration a reasonable size and the volume of work involved roughly the same from year to year. Sales are always stumpage ones, in other words, the prices are agreed while the trees are still standing and the buyer sees to the harvesting.

Competition in the area is good from the owner's point of view. Eine Rosenberg asks for quotations from three big forest companies and two large sawmills and then chooses one. The agreement, in which price is the prime factor, may often cover two or three years. "I see that over the past ten years I've sold to three different companies," she says. Although in sales such as this the labour consideration is not the seller's problem, I ask her to give a moment's thought to the effect of her forests on the employment situation.

"During the summer one logger will work through the sapling stands in the space of about two months. Planting in the spring accounts for about two man-weeks. If necessary I can do the sowing myself. The average volume sold per year is two thousand cubic metres, which means two men will have to spend about one week in the forest with a harvester." A little simple arithmetic shows that forty lorry-loads of wood leave these forests for the mills each year.

We city folk tend to imagine that timber deals are clinched in a central-heated office or a room at the manor used only for entertaining guests, and that the owner and his wife need never set foot inside the actual forest. Is this true? "There are all sorts of ways of going about it," I am informed. "Before signing anything, I always want to see for myself personally, because there may be minor considerations to allow for in the price. Nature may have sprung a surprise since I last visited that particular neck of the woods. Nature is not a museum; it is a living organism renewing all the time."

What, then, does nature mean to the forest-owner?
"Once the wood has been harvested, I want the landscape to look vigorous, so some things have to be thought out case by case. There are certain areas of my forests I do not want to touch, but it annoys me if I am ordered to do something to them. The instructions are all so standardised, as if people have worked them out on a computer.

Take the protection zones nowadays obligatory in littoral areas. Sometimes they look simply dreadful. It would be better to clear them away altogether."

Members of Finland's nouveau riche have over the past few years, been investing their newly-gained wealth in country estates, forests and land in general and by no means always in their own companies. This comes as no surprise to Eine Rosenberg. "New money finds its way into old, established industries. I am, however, a little concerned at the eagerness of old forest companies to sell their own forests. I just hope their explanations – that it will mean they can concentrate more on their core business – turns out to be correct."

Later, in Helsinki, I meet a different kind of forest-owner. He visits his forests only once or twice a summer, and never in winter. For him, forests are an investment in the same way as real estate or shares on the stock market, and he leaves their care and assessment entirely in the hands of experts.

Risto Sarpiola is a chartered accountant by profession – a man who, in his own words, may not know much about silviculture but is a wizard with the figures with which he works. He also has other investments and has been a forest-owner for only a few years. "Forest is one of the most reliable investments. It keeps growing, especially if it's looked after, and it yields compound interest. It grows so slowly, however, that my wife and I won't benefit much from the family's investments, but one day our son will find himself drowning in timber," he laughs.

▶ One generation gives way to the next, but life in the forests goes on. It has long been a tradition in agrarian society to try to leave the estate in a better condition than that in which it was received.

▲ **Lands for the landless were usually carved out of state forests. This policy prevented social unrest in Finland.**

"The family bought up four forest plots and now own about 400 hectares in southeast Finland. We gradually warmed to the idea of becoming forest-owners. Maybe we were just a little sentimental, too. My wife's home farm was in Karelia, the area lost to the Russians as a result of the war. As an accountant, I was familiar with forest taxation, so when a forest plot of a hundred hectares just happened to come up for sale near our summer cottage, the decision to buy it was an easy one."

The urban forest-owner is not, however, without a streak of the nature-lover in him and confesses to getting totally intoxicated by the beauty of a forest or marsh, ants, the fragrance of cranberry blossom and birdsong on the few occasions he does venture out into the forest. "There are some Natura areas right near us. We've managed to come to an agreement with the people from the Ministry of the Environment on all the things that really matter," says the satisfied investor.

Ever since he bought his first forest plot, Risto Sarpiola has placed his trust in the local forestry people, who have assessed the quality and quantity of the timber and decided what needs to be done in the forest. "When it comes to doing business, I'm on home ground again. I'm good at negotiating and bargaining." The reliable silviculture expert is, in his opinion, the best consultant. "By following his advice I know I am looking after my property, and I've had nothing to complain about."

As in so many lines of business, the lower the purchase price, the higher the yield. Forest land tends to come on the market when legacies are divided up and couples get divorced. Sometimes forest is sold when the next generation goes away to study and needs somewhere to live in the university town.

A typical Finnish forest-owner, and there are some 300,000 of them, is Kaarlo Immonen from Varpaisjärvi, a farmer and harvester contractor for whom forest owner-

◀ Forestry is one way of ensuring that all parts of the country stay inhabited. The village schools guarantees a safe start to life.

HH

LR

LR

ship is not the main source of income but very much a way of life. Half the home farm of less than thirty hectares is forest and accounts at best for no more than a tenth of Immonen's income. "I inherited standard Finnish forest and I tend and harvest it myself. Sometimes a neighbour comes and helps me plant, but I do the felling and drive the logs to the roadside on my own."

For tax reasons Immonen says he sells a little timber every year. He couldn't live without his forest. He needs enough to maintain a feeling for nature and forestry. The annual cycle means a lot to him.

Would he sell if a neighbour came along and made him an offer? "No way!" he replies, without a moment's hesitation.

◀ **Kaarlo Immonen from Varpaisjärvi wants to own some forest though it's not his main occupation. Silviculture is an important factor in life for him.**

CUSTODIANS OF THE FOREST

"HE THAT PLANTS TREES LOVES OTHERS BESIDES HIM-self," says an English proverb. Although wood provides a livelihood for more than five million Europeans, and everyone is in daily contact with products derived from it, forests are no longer a presence for many urban members of society.

How about those entrusted with the custody of Finland's national asset? How do they see the forests and nature? On what values, and what cultural heritage do they base their day-to-day decisions? The six gentlemen I interviewed are focal figures in Finland's forest industry. Two of them own a moderate chunk of forest, three small plots adjoining their summer cottages.

▶ **Jan Heino, Director-General of Metsähallitus, the Finnish state forest enterprise, custodian of Finland's largest forest reserves, has to get back to his roots from time to time. He needs to keep in touch to be able to tell foreigners about Finland's forest management.**

LR

Jan Heino, Director-General of Metsähallitus, the Finnish state forest enterprise, does not own a single hectare of forest. "It's not for lack of opportunity," he says. "The first came when my parents decided to retire. Since I had a degree in forestry, my bank manager was sure I would be dying to get my hands on the family forests. However, I felt that the viability of the home farm of just under 30 hectares under cultivation and the same amount of forest would be endangered if we split it up. So the farm went to my brother, remained intact, and to my delight has since grown."

The bulk of Finland's protected area is on Metsähallitus land. Steward of the country's biggest forest assets, Metsähallitus does not regard its job as simply to protect the environment or the nation's recreational resources. "The state is Finland's biggest forest-owner and thus a major employer. It's up to us to see that there is work for log-

LR

gers in the rural regions and a supply of timber for the sawmills," Heino says.

Hans Gutzeit was a large Norwegian sawmill-owner when he came to Finland in the late 19th century and founded a sawmill in Kotka. In no time the little town on the south coast had become the biggest sawmill centre in the country. In 1918, after Finland had become an independent republic the sawmill was purchased by the state and entered into an alliance with the Enso sawmill supplied by the forests of the Saimaa lake region. This was just one of a chain of ownership and structural changes in the forest industry of Finland and Sweden that in 1998 gave rise to the company Stora Enso, now the world's second largest producer of paper and board.

Stora Enso President and CEO Jukka Härmälä owns enough forest to keep the family in sauna firewood. "I own about five hectares of forest at my summer place. It's enough in the sense that I have to fill in an annual farm tax return form. When it comes to harvesting, I rely on people trained to do the job." Stora Enso has its head office in Helsinki, but its international office is in London not far from the streets and clubs where the first agreements on trading in paper and wood, Finland's green gold, with the rest of the world were signed.

Juha Niemelä, President and CEO of the world's number six forest industry company, UPM-Kymmene, has only a couple of hectares of forest to his name, around his home and his summer cottage. He thus spends little time managing his own forests, but all the more shouldering his com-

◀ Stora Enso has its head office in Helsinki, but President and CEO Jukka Härmälä spends a lot of his time at the company's international office in London.

◀ UPM-Kymmene's President and CEO Juha Niemelä is crazy about football and takes corporate visitors to watch Valkeakosken Haka play.

LR

pany's social responsibility. UPM-Kymmene has donated or undertaken to protect 1,700 hectares of forest in the Repovesi wilderness area in Southeast Finland. With the forests owned by the state, the result is a national park with an area of nearly 3,000 hectares.

UPM-Kymmene's most recent achievement in the cultural domain is the art exhibition "The Spirit of the Forest" held at the Kunsthalle in Helsinki in autumn 2001. On exhibition were 120 of the finest works in the company's collection. "The collection is a larger-than-usual treasure trove," was the comment of the art expert who put the exhibition together. Niemelä is crazy about football. The small mill town has for decades boasted a team that in its prime played against the top European clubs. Whenever possible, Niemelä takes his corporate visitors to watch a Valkeakosken Haka match."

Antti Oksanen, President and CEO of the Metsäliitto Group, has a few trees registered in his name, but again he uses his forest only for his supply of firewood. "I've usually got a trailer attached to my quad bike." Oksanen does, however, keep an eye on the 20 hectares of forest inherited by his wife. "With her permission," he laughs. Oksanen is another football fan. The Group (listing at no. 12 in the world) once had a chance to prove itself and its social responsibility by building a stadium for the Finnish championship league team Atlantis. The stands, of wooden construction, are worth going to see even when play is not in progress.

◀ **Antti Oksanen, President and CEO of the Metsäliitto Group, is holding an angle gauge, made of all the species of wood found in Finland, such as is awarded to Forest Academy graduates.**

LR

MTK, the Central Union of Agricultural Producers and Forest-Owners, is the primary lobby for forest-owners in Finland. Its President, Esa Härmälä, is the owner of 200 hectares in Southwest Finland. "I make all the decisions affecting my forest according to a forest plan that the forest management association later implements. Sometimes I go out into the forest myself, tidying up the roadsides and things." In one respect Härmälä is an out and out city man. The Union's headquarters, at what roughly translates as "Country House", have always been in the very heart of Helsinki and there is no intention to move them anywhere else.

LR

▲ **Markku Koskinen, director of Koskisen Oy, practises what he preaches. The textbooks used at the polytechnic operating under the company's auspices were produced at Koskisen.**

Markku Koskinen, director of Koskisen Oy, has his feet firmly planted in the forest and actually lives on his 200-hectare forest estate in Southern Finland. "The silviculture is taken care of under agreement by Koskitukki Oy. I take a fairly active part in planning both the felling to be done and the silviculture measures. I don't actually work in the forest myself, apart from collecting firewood and doing an occasional bit of clearing." The company is extremely proud of its apprenticeship system, its own internal vocational school that even produces the textbooks it needs. Hardly surprisingly the staff turnover is slight.

When I ask these forest stewards what aspects of Finnish forestry they find most difficult to explain to foreigners, I am not surprised by their replies. "Most people visiting Finland for the first time seem very surprised to discover that so much of Finland really is covered by forest," says Jukka Härmälä. "They expect to see little fields with trees in them. Time and time again I also have to explain the harvesting processes. I have my job cut out to explain the importance of silviculture measures and thinning for the growth of the trees and the forest yield. I also have to be prepared to explain the universal right to wander through the forests and pick the berries and mushrooms growing there."

According to Antti Oksanen, some first-time visitors fail to grasp the importance of forestry to the Finnish economy. "In Central and Southern Europe the forests are not family-owned the way they are in Finland. People here take it for granted that you look after your forest. You use it economically, but you also tend it every year. The forests are a vital source of additional income for thousands and thousands of farmers."

The most common source of amazement, in Markku Koskinen's experience, is the structure of Finland's forest ownership, which differs from that in many other countries. "Ownership is private and small-scale, and even small plots of forest may be an important source of income to the owner. This in itself guarantees that the owners look after the environment and don't overdo clear cutting. But it isn't easy to get this across to the Central European."

Esa Härmälä has lost count of the number of times he has explained how the Finns have used their forests ever since the ice receded 10,000 years ago. "A hundred years ago, during the era of slash-and-burn cultivation and tar

LR

burning, the forests got much rougher treatment. Today the Finnish forests are 'managed natural forests'. They also keep themselves in trim."

▲ Like all forest-owners, Esa Härmälä takes pleasure in counting the growth rings on trees felled on his own land.

The idea that the Finnish forests cannot be depleted by harvesting is alien to many of Antti Oksanen's guests and clients. "If you just leave a field and don't do anything to it, in a year's time it'll be waist-high with trees." Juha Niemelä has found that foreigners sometimes wonder why there is any argument about the forests. Jan Heino says he has heard similar comments. "My foreign colleagues often

LR

wonder why Finland's forest management and Metsähallitus come in for such severe criticism. Forest experts familiar with practices in different countries say the way we treat our forests stands out as an example to others. They cannot relate the criticism they have heard to what they have seen in Finland."

This is something Heino himself has difficulty in understanding. Maybe forestry is so important in Finland that its status as an institution makes feelings run high. And the criticism makes itself heard far afield. "Another difficult thing," he says "is describing our forestry organisation. Providing a clear overall picture is not easy. Because it's such an important industry, we have so many organisations."

The bureaucracy has, in Heino's opinion, lessened since the organisations receiving government aid were streamlined and their number somewhat reduced. "There are, however, still certain aspects of both the legislation and organisation of the forest sector that can be explained to people from another culture with only time and patience. For me it's a pleasant job, because I can feel proud of the excellent results achieved in Finland."

The custodians of the forest unanimously agree that the environmentalists are sometimes right in their criticism. "There is always something to be learned from criticism, however radical," says Jukka Härmälä. "An international player in this field cannot simply sit back and let things take their course. Thanks to the environmentalists far more thought has been given over the past few years to the nesting conditions for birds, the timing of harvesting, rotten trees and controlled burning."

◄ **Esa Härmälä, President of the Central Union of Agricultural Producers and Forest-Owners (MTK), has personal experience of both tending the forests and hunting the game in them.**

▶ In Finland you camp for a short while on someone else's land, but the owner's permission of the owner is needed to light a fire. The Jyrävä falls in Kuusamo.

Juha Niemelä praises the environmentalists for their biodiversity concern, as does Markku Koskinen: "The environmentalists have made a big thing of biodiversity. The forest industry itself has done a good job in ensuring that the forests are not over-harvested, but, despite the occasional excesses, the preservation of biodiversity has guaranteed better potential for the versatile use of the forests."

Antti Oksanen claims that the Finnish mills and other production plants place less strain on the environment than almost any others in the world. "Maybe the environmentalists have made us more aware of and sensitive to this issue as well." Esa Härmälä nevertheless feels that the environmentalists sometimes tend to forget things that the forest industry cannot overlook. "Sustainable development does not just mean ecological sustainability but economic and social sustainability too."

Jan Heino seconds this: "The environmentalists have been given credit for lots of things. Even as far back as the 19th century forestry was already adopting the principle, but the concept has changed and broadened as our knowledge increases and new research is carried out." Heino also raises his hat to the environmentalists for championing biodiversity. "On the other hand, in recent years they have sometimes clearly gone too far and forgotten economic and social sustainability."

The forest bosses all admit to being great nature-lovers. Juha Niemelä skis, enjoys being out on the water and roaming through the forest. Antti Oksanen and Esa Härmälä are keen hunters and are familar with all forms

LR

of the sport. Oksanen also fishes, as does Jukka Härmälä: "I have been out in the forest and on the sea all my life and really enjoy it. When I was young, I would spend ages bird-watching, and I still try to find time to follow the great spring migrations in May. Each year it seems more breath-taking."

Markku Koskinen used to be an active Boy Scout: "I still like being out in the forest and even spending the night there. Nowadays I go either on foot or on a snow-mobile, but I also drive a quad bike and a tractor. I like fishing and boating, too, but my wife has refused to take me berry-picking ever since I once wanted to take my chainsaw with me. Every now and then – the whole family goes out on a 'forest expedition'. We ramble together and enjoy a picnic in the depths of the country."

Jan Heino is another keen hunter, berry and mushroom picker, and angler. "The forest is a part of me and a part of my family's life. I've noticed that it takes time to form a picture of the vast forests owned by the state. I plan my schedule so that I can also use my free time to get to know new areas. I find it mentally refreshing to get out in the countryside, where time stands still. And my ability to do my job properly improves as I get to know our flora and fauna better."

There is one thing that worries Esa Härmälä more than any other: "Being spokesman for our forest-owners, I sometimes ask myself in amazement why we have had no qualms about slapping protection orders on hundreds of thousands of hectares of forest and taking them out of production. Forestry should still be a growth industry." Härmälä sees two external threats: one is the action taken by Finland itself, and the other is Russia. "Our wood-processing industry is a global business. Unless Finland can guarantee an operating environment sufficiently favourable, companies will draw their own conclusions. Russia's forest resources are 40 times those of Finland, but the volume harvested only twice as much. Now there is potential!"

The Bible says: *"For there is hope of a tree, if it be cut down, that it will sprout again, and that the tender branch thereof will not cease."* (Job 14:7)

THE HUNTER'S FOREST

EARLY MORNING IN AUTUMN, AND THE FOREST IS fragrant with heather, pine needles and freshly-fallen leaves. The huntsman's boot leaves footprints on the withering grass and moss while the firs sprinkle raindrops down his neck. Worm-eaten mushrooms, reduced to pulp by the heavy tread, merge with the slippery, rotting leaves. The freezing breath of man and dog softens the rays of a sun hanging low in the sky. Yet this is the time, as nature yields to the icy grip of winter, that the forest has most to offer.

Throughout most of the European heartlands hunting is a sport confined to the upper or upper-middle classes. Only on the periphery is it still a source of amusement or livelihood regardless of rank or status. Sympathy with the hunted is thus greatest in the major cities of Europe. Yet for the Finns, stewards of a large country on the continent's northern border, hunting is as natural a pursuit as cycling is for the Dutch. Just the fact of being out in the forest means far more to many than the game that they are hunting. Subject to strict control, hunting requires a permit. The police keep a strict record of rifles and hunting clubs check that their members really know how to use them. Not just anyone can go out hunting for anything or anywhere.

In a country with a population of five million, no fewer than 300,000 men and a few thousand women belong to a hunting club. Elk-hunting permits, for example, are issued only to hunting clubs. Since all members have at least one rifle, and many several, Finland is in one sense a country armed to the teeth. It does, however, differ from American society in that we use our rifles purely for hunting and not for self-defence. Unless, of course, there happens to be a national crisis...

LR

▶ **Elks just love a juicy seedling, and hunters a meaty elk.**

I personally have two guns, a shotgun and an elk rifle, and licences for both. This does not mean I head for the forest every weekend like some keen hunters I know. So far there are still more hunters in Finland than golfers, though the balance is shifting all the time. My shotgun is an old Russian "Baikal", the Lada of the shotgun world and can, if called upon, double as a crowbar. The elk rifle is far more up-market: a 1980s Sako. It has a beautiful hand-engraved butt and above the barrel is a smeary old sight that has saved the life of many an elk.

Now elk hunting, if anything, is a ritual, an ordered, 'back-to-nature' sortie from the civilised world when the year is on the decline. Naturally it no longer has anything whatsoever to do with finding food for the family. The row of diesel four-by-fours by the roadside is a sure sign that different social classes are engaging in dialogue over a communal campfire for the next few days or so. The locals will be up and heating the hunting lodges and saunas while the city gents are still buying their designer sweaters to go under their hunting suits. Once the hunt is on, the locals, who are familiar with the terrain, will be able to predict how the animals will behave and advise the townsfolk on the best place to wait.

Here again the forest is the common denominator. The decisive factor at play is the atavistic pull felt by urbanised man to savour the wood smoke of a fire deep in the forest, at the mercy of nature, so to speak, though the nearest doctor may be just round the corner and he can call up a taxi at any time on his mobile. For deep within the human soul is a burning desire to hunt. Since no one hunts to eat these

LR

days, it is no longer a question of life or death when the huntsman sights an elk. Yet even the old hand's pulse will quicken, he will catch his breath, his hands will sweat and he will become deaf to all the other sounds around him. The cold that only a moment before seemed to chill his very bones is no more than a distant memory. His first thought as the shot echoes round the forest is one of incredulous joy: I actually did it! The elk takes a step or two before stumbling to its knees and crashing to the ground. Did I hit the leg or the head? If it was the leg, I'm in for some serious joshing at the party tonight.

Once the elk is hit, the locals set about the messy business, skinning the animal and chopping up the meat to be delivered vacuum-packed in meal-sized portions to the gallant company later in the day. The price per kilo of meat thus procured falls little short of that of caviar, but what price is the urban dweller not prepared to pay for an adventure such as this? The meat in the soup at the party tonight will probably have been bagged at the previous hunt. The locals will go home with the impression of a merry band of men and a good supply of stories with which to regale their friends. The profitability of the adventure tour will be reflected in the tax returns of the village proprietors.

Most hunting parties, however, are made up of ordinary local residents or colleagues, and an increasing number of women bitten by the hunting bug. And when the hunt is over, the soup bubbling in the pot and the calf liver sizzling in the pan, the womenfolk will be more than welcome to join in. The hierarchy during the hunt is the same as on board ship: there is only one captain. The most experienced huntsman is put in charge, and his word is law. Each mem-

◄ Safety is very impor-
tant during the hunt. The
best place to wait for an
elk is a tower: the visibil-
ity is good but the aim is
at the ground.

▼ Quiz question: how
many elks can you spot
in the picture overleaf?

175

► A wood grouse (*Tetrao urogallus*) is a greatly prized catch. The grouse population has diminished for many reasons, and restrictions on shooting have been imposed in recent years.

LR

► A perfect day for hunting. The hound has flushed a hare and the men have bagged some hazel grouse (*Bonasia bonasia*) as well.

ber of the hunt must be able to produce a valid gun licence and demonstrate his or her skill with a rifle before the hunt can begin.

Hunting is a good school for teaching men at least the meaning of a natural pecking order. It is a sport that calls for certain social skills that have – so far – served them well in defending their patch in the gender battle. For when necessity calls, they are able to band together in the combat against a greater common foe, which in this case happens to be an elk. The unschooled local farmer will issue pistol-shot orders to the captain of industry, who meekly obeys because he knows that at precisely that moment, and in precisely that situation he has neither the knowledge nor know-how needed to fell his prey. It's a sort of "peasant as king" situation. Once the animal has been bagged and the chops and steaks packed in polythene, the roles will be reversed. These role games must, surely, serve some purpose, otherwise hunting would not be so popular.

LR

LR

LR   LR

Elk hunting in fact satisfies two needs in society. First, elks are a real danger on Finnish roads, and second, they cause havoc to saplings in the forest. As a result, few question the number of permits issued. By contrast, there is constant wrangling in the press over the number of permits to hunt wolves and bears. Most Finns nowadays seem to be increasingly in favour of culling these, too, as more and more cross the border from Russia and encroach on farms and villages.

The season for the most common game birds, wood grouse, black grouse, hazel grouse and willow grouse, runs from mid-September to the end of October. In Northern and Eastern Finland in particular, grouse-shooting is a popular sport, promising a welcome addition to the larder. Since grouse-shooting also requires a dog, the equation is clear: the family is sick of hamburgers and pizzas and the dog needs some exercise, so dad must get out in the forest. What a wonderful excuse! "One of the best things about hunting," said a certain 19th century Russian landowner,

◄ **Finnish women are invading yet another domain traditionally reserved for men.**

LR

"is that it entails constant travelling from one estate to another, which is such a delightful way of passing the time."

Some gentlemen with pretentious inclinations have developed a taste for pheasant-shooting. A tendency to sneer and to denounce the beating of semi-tame birds as little short of butchery seems to be particularly prevalent among those denied the pleasure. This image was certainly not burnished by a hunting trip some years ago in which the members of the shooting party included the President of Finland and the King of Sweden. The bag? Over six-hundred pheasants and a magpie. The popularity of dogs is explained by the simple fact that even the most stupid of dog-owners is cleverer than his dog. A dog is also wiser than a woman, say the Russians: "They do not yap at their master."

Duck-shooting begins each year in Finland sharp at noon on August 20. All of a sudden shots can be heard in all directions. Round our lake duck-shooting begins ten minutes later, as the feathered refugees from nearby lakes seek political asylum on ours. For some obscure reason waterfowl do not have the wit to seek shelter in the forest. At the start of the duck-shooting season the newspapers receive a steady stream of letters to the editor complaining about shot raining down on someone's summer cottage or a neighbour rat-tat-tatting with a shotgun even after dusk has fallen. The most common accident during the duck-shooting season is, however, drowning – the duck shooter.

Personally I prefer hunting hares, especially on a cold, frosty day with the sun is shining, when it is half science,

◀ **August 20 is an important day in Finland. The shots echoing around the reedy lakeshores are a sign that the duck-shooting season has begun.**

▶ **The owner's pride and joy. The more decorative the stock, the better.**

LR

half art. The locals have excellent hounds that sooner or later drive long-ears within aiming distance. The hare may be hundreds of metres ahead of the dog, but experienced huntsmen can predict from the dog's barking where the hare will go. I recall one occasion when I was advised: "You'll be able to shoot from there. Don't move an inch." Easier said than done when the temperature is –20 or more. A couple of hours later, hearing a dog bark in a completely different quarter, I took a few steps in that direction, at which the barking stopped. And what did I find on returning to my hideout? Fresh hare tracks all around it in the snow.

▶ **The bear is king of the Finnish forests and bear-hunting the sport of kings. More permits have been issued as the bear population has grown. Almost a hundred bears are shot in Finland each year.**

Nations have the same preconceived ideas about others' sports and business practices as they do about their food, religions and toilet habits. The Europeans criticise whale-hunting in Japan, but a Japanese acquaintance of

► **A recipe (overleaf) used by Ari Ruoho, chef at the Alexander Nevski restaurant in Helsinki.**

mine cannot fathom how anyone could eat veal, the off-spring of a cow. The moralising northerners are all for prohibiting bull fights in Spain and small bird netting in Italy, while southerners look upon seal and bear-hunting as barbarian. Hunting has such a long history in Finland that marten and squirrel pelts were once the currency of barter trade.

In my capacity as journalist I have even been fox hunt-ing with members of the gentry in southern England. As a form of theatre it was slightly ridiculous, but it never-theless had a certain charm and displayed a fine sense of ritual. The fox does not warrant our compassion: it has far crueller enemies in nature than packs of hounds and gen-tlemen on horseback. Its worst enemy is in fact the com-bustion engine. The complacent sport of an upper class decked out in red coats offers thousands of farmers a wel-come chance to eke out the family income. Many of the most vociferous opponents are people who have never had a chance to take part themselves, either on horseback or on foot. And they, of course, constitute the majority.

It is widely recognised that in every Member State the rural region inhabitants are by far the most suspicious of the communal goals and practices of the European Union. This is hardly surprising, seeing that the orders are issued by a central authority making no allowance for local cus-toms and traditions, and that the Brussels bureaucrats pur-sue a policy of dictation that differs little from that with which the Kremlin once terrorised the Soviet citizen. As a rule the orders have nothing whatsoever to do with the free movement of people, goods, services and capital; they are chaff churned out by a bureaucratic mill and serve to

LR

Stuffed fillet of elk

600 g of fillet of elk
Stuffing:
100 g wheat bread
100 g wild mushrooms
2 garlic cloves
parsley
butter
salt and white pepper

Roasting net (pig's stomach)

Dice the bread and fry in butter. Fry the mushrooms with the garlic. Stir in the chopped parsley and leave to cool.

Season the elk with salt and pepper. Place the stuffing between the fillets and form into a rold. Insert the roll in the net with the help of cling film. Store in a cold place for six hours. Brown the meat in a pan and roast in the oven for about 10 min. Leave to stand wrapped in a towel for about 20 min. before carving.

Rosemary sauce

4 dl game sauce
a few sprigs of fresh rosemary

Heat the sauce and add the rosemary. Remove the saucepan from the heat, cover and leave to stand for a few hours. Strain before serving.

Rosemary potatoes

3 good-sized potatoes
2 dl clarified butter
a few sprigs of fresh rosemary

Heat the butter and rosemary. Bake the potatoes in their skins in the oven (200 oC for about 1 hour). Hollow them out and mix the potato with the butter. Season with salt and white pepper. Place the creamed potato in a dish and bake for a further 25 min or so. Cut into pieces when cool.

estrange people the length and breadth of the continent from the noble objectives of a united Europe. Hunting is part of a national tradition and should thus enjoy the same protection as any other endangered species.

During the Cold War, when western Europe laboured under the misconception that Finland lay the wrong side of the Iron Curtain, a friend of mine was driving an American acquaintance round Finland when they arrived at the scene of an accident caused by an elk. Luckily this time no one was hurt, but a large bull elk was still gasping its last beside the road. The police had not yet arrived so my friend went and fetched his elk rifle from the boot of his car, put the animal out of its misery and drove off. The American was looking a little pale, and half an hour passed before he ventured to stutter, "Do you Finns always keep a rifle in the trunk?" At which my friend, by that time fed up with the American's insinuations about Finlandisierung, replied, "We have to."

WOOD CRAFT

SCULPTOR PAUNO POHJOLAINEN HAS A STUDIO redolent of a carpenter's workshop, of turpentine and paint. The pony-tailed artist is hard at work, a slightly pained expression on his face. He is busy; his next exhibition is looming near and for that he needs something new. A visitor, however, is not to be dismissed without a welcome, for he may have come to buy something, or to bring glad tidings of a spectacular prize or award.

Pohjolainen was named Finnish Artist of the Year in 1997, the year in which he received the *Ars Fennica* prize. Explaining the reason for its choice the committee said that, using traditional methods and traditional carpenter's and painter's tools, he had succeeded in creating modern art that transcends national borders.

LR

LR

The material Pohjolainen has chosen to work with is wood, an extremely challenging, difficult material loved by Finnish amateur artists from time immemorial. During lulls in the fighting in WWII troops would while away the hours whittling cups and bowls and ghastly tea sets out of gnarled wood. Lumberjacks with an artistic streak would use their chainsaws to carve rude figures out of quirky tree-trunks. Even the carvings made by professional artists are too reminiscent of those sold as genuine African art in market places the world over.

▲ Pauno Pohjolainen's large sculptures demand a large studio. Works this size are usually bought for public buildings.

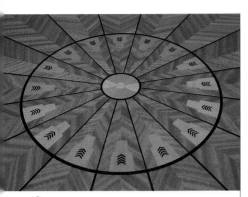

LR

Here, though, is an artist who has discovered in wood dimensions not necessarily obvious to the layman. Moulding and breaking up the natural surface of the material to suit the workings of his mind, he constructs optical illusions, changes the perspective with saw and glue, and combines his wood with other materials. Any remaining boundaries he then dispels with colour, so that by the time he has finished, the viewer may have difficulty deciding whether the works are paintings or sculptures. His work reflects the influence of both Frank Stella and Vincent van Gogh, and the critics claim to see points in common with Paul Klee and Wassily Kandinsky. Pohjolainen is the first Finnish wood sculptor to adopt a clearly universal idiom.

Right now the artist is fired by motifs of Orthodox and Byzantine art and the forms they inspire. The light is refracted on the surface to create purple, gold and black. The original wood shade is overlaid with silver or illuminated in medieval style. As one experienced critic extolled, his art exudes a sense of great mystery and inexplicable beauty.

The higher the degree of conversion, the better the price per kilo. Whereas a kilo of sawn timber can be purchased for half a euro, paper and board cost almost one euro, a wooden table 10 euros and a Rapala wooden fish lure 500 euros a kilo.

Fifty kilometres from Pohjolainen lives another craftsman – a man originally from another culture. Lutz Reinhardt was born into a doctor's family in Stuttgart, Germany some fifty years ago but has been living in Finland for just on thirty. He has received numerous awards for his work to revive the Finnish carpentry tradition.

▶ **For decades now furniture for Finland's embassies has been made in a little Finnish country village. The Lutz Reinhardt company has exclusive rights in Finland to the manufacture of furniture designed by Eliel Saarinen.**

194

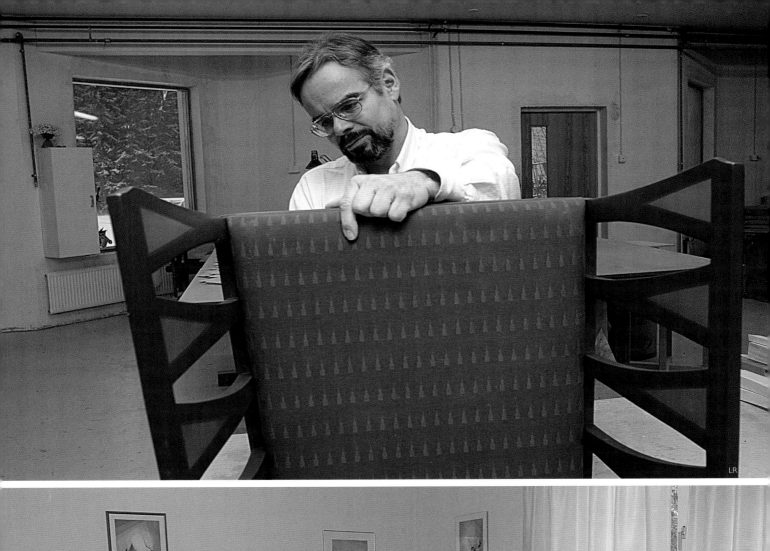

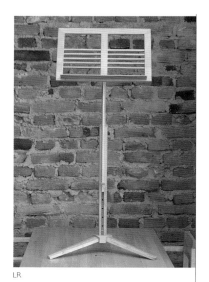

LR

▲ **This music stand in black alder was made by Markku Eertola from Lahden Pro Puu.**

Another foreigner who is teaching the Finns how to use their own material!

The team founded and led by Reinhardt produces hand-made period furniture and musical instruments. It took a pedantic German to put works of art created a hundred years ago by Eliel Saarinen back into circulation. Finland's embassies can thus now show the world furniture that was for decades out of production: those in Berlin, London, New York, Brussels, Singapore and Tallinn furnish their guest rooms with tables and chairs lovingly made of wood and literally in the middle of the forest.

Reinhardt has no desire to operate on a vast industrial scale. Instead, he and his apprentices make unique products for customers who can appreciate their quality and afford to pay for it. On display at the Frankfurt hi-fi fair were amplifiers made of wood and costing fiventhousand euros a pair. Musical instruments are close to Reinhardt's heart. He himself plays classical music but feels quite at home with rock. "Under the guidance of the Finnish instrument-maker Aarno Pelto we have made dozens of unique instruments here, harpsichords, clavichords and virginals using rosewood, flame birch, red beech, linden, pine, oak, flame alder and maple. The harmony of wood and music is simply heavenly!"

Nowhere is this more audible than in the Sibelius Hall in Lahti. Music, in counterpoint with the quality wood grown by forest owners and supplied by industry, has joined with the builder's art to create a concert hall like no other. A century and a half ago some go-ahead businessmen founded a steam sawmill beside Lake Vesijärvi to convert the logs floated down from the north. Thirty years later

LR

► Hannu Liukkonen, many times winner of the Sulkava rowing race, makes racing boats, church boats and ordinary wooden boats in the workshop on his farm.

LR

LR

LR

LR

Jean Sibelius travelled by train to Lahti and boarded a boat to cross the lake to a villa where he could compose in peace. Alongside the old sawmill today stands a music centre in which new technology combines with all the wood know-how the Finns sacrificed for decades to that material known as concrete.

The foyer of the Sibelius Hall is called the Forest Hall. Covering a thousand square metres, it is big and high enough to accommodate a five-storey block of flats. The roof rafters and struts are evocative of trees and branches. The walls are glass, and the lake over which Sibelius once gazed sparkles before the concert-goer's eyes. Architects Hannu Tikka and Kimmo Lintula like to explain their

◀ **The Trojan Horse sculpted in wood by Mauno Hartman outside the Sibelius Hall in Lahti. The Hall's reception desk is faced with birchbark.**

201

LR

► **Conductor Osmo Vänskä is delighted and honoured to rehearse the Lahti Symphony Orchestra in the the Sibelius Hall's superb acoustics.**

LR

▶ Kirkniemi in Lohja was once the home of Finland's Marshal Mannerheim – just one of the illustrious owners in the history of the estate.

design by comparing it to nature. The Finnish forest has a calming effect, as does the presence of water.

The concert and congress hall can seat over a thousand, and boasts acoustics pronounced nothing short of excellent. This may explain why the Sibelius Hall has suddenly become the Finland's number one recording studio. The colour scheme, the way the wooden surfaces are used and the shape of the hall recall a giant violin or cello. It is as if the listener is sitting inside an instrument made of precious wood, in all the fullness of sound.

Conductors, musicians and critics are unanimous in claiming that the Sibelius Hall is one of the finest concert halls in the world. It is certainly one of the best in Finland. "It makes the music sound warm," says conductor Osmo Vänskää of his home base. "The warmth in the sound brings out the cellos and violas and makes the music infinitely enjoyable."

Is wood the secret behind it all? "It does help to account for the perfect acoustics, but the shape of the hall is the most important factor. The 'shoebox' concert hall has proved to be the best. Which is why Russell Johnson designed us a hall this shape, along the lines of Vienna, Amsterdam and Boston. And thanks to the clever use of wood, the strings, in particular, as wooden instruments, sound really beautiful here."

The Metsäliitto Group played a decisive role in seeing that the football stadium at Myyrmäki in Vantaa, just north of Helsinki, was made of wood. The wood in the stands here is not just ornamental, since everything, from the bearing structures to the interior, has been made on the material's terms. Ideas for the wooden seats were imported

from abroad. The Pohjola Stadium is a 'friendly' sports arena for a few thousand spectators and a fine source of inspiration to the teams and athletes who use it.

Tradition, culture and sustainable development are not by definition mutually exclusive. In summer 2002 the Metsäliitto Group became owner of the Kirkniemi estate in Lohja. The wooden manor house dates from the 18th century and is in neo-classical style. It became known to the Finns as the last home of their great military hero, Marshal C.G.E. Mannerheim.

In autumn 2001 UPM-Kymmene purchased the more than 150 year-old Haindl paper mill in Germany. "Haindl was founded in 1849 in the Kingdom of Bavaria. It survived as a family business throughout the Weimar Republic, the Nazi regime and the Federal German Republic – but it has failed to withstand the pressures of globalisation," wrote Die Zeit.

◀ **The Metsäliitto Group bought the Kirkniemi estate in 2000. It is now a meeting place for Finnish and foreign corporate visitors. Situated not far from the Kirkniemi Paper Mill of M-Real, a member of the Metsäliitto Group, it is perfect for entertaining.**

LR

OUR COMMUNAL GARDEN

THE TRAVELLER NEVER RETURNS, OR SO IT IS CLAIMED, more stupid than when he set out. Until I embarked on this book, forest ownership was to me a remote occupation confined to country folk, the forest industry something people traded in on the stock exchange, and forests a resource that renewed itself of its own accord.

If you want to preserve your preconceived ideas it is fatal to start anything. This applies to both things and people. At the beginning of this book I described how I happened to notice a similarity between the gardens of Europe and the Finnish forests. As I wrote, I learnt that silviculture is ideally a systematic undertaking in which nothing is left to chance. Nature alone is capable of springing surprises.

Land ownership always calls forth strong emotions. Peasants the world over are suspicious of city folk. The taxmen, politicians and civil servants are urban institutions and represent The Government. One thing Communism taught us, if nothing else, is that people look after their personal possessions better than society's. The sanctity of the right of ownership is indeed one of the pillars of the European market economy. Hence, the forest-owner is particular about his property.

Owning forest is a long-term commitment. It sometimes amuses me to read in the papers about new money being invested in land, forests and country houses rather than in the new technologies. On closer reflection, it is, of course, wise to anchor part of one's future on ground inherited and tested in practice. What's more, it is in our national interest. Forest is a national asset.

The entire forest industry chain – the forest cluster, as it is fashionably called – is far better than it is reputed to be, yet it has received little praise in the past few years. The voices of those who, as they tread the city streets, join in outcry against Finland's forest policy have been louder than the voices of those speaking in its defence, and have carried further afield.

The Finnish forestry is justified in commanding respect yet under obligation to pay society its due. We may well demand of the industry that, as it grows and becomes increasingly global, it universally applies the same principles of sustainable development as those in force in Finland. Our mill communities, whether they be in Windsorlock, USA, Augsburg in Germany or Kuusankoski in Finland have long traditions, in both production and the field of culture.

One of the cherished principles of the single European market is free mobility of people, commodities, capital and services. The Union founders would be astonished if, from beyond the grave, they could see just how far integration has gone in the space of fifty years. The future of the continent must not, however, be endangered by decisions that fail to make allowance for the individual interests of the regions.

All Europeans, regardless of where they live, have a right to a good life in the occupation or calling of either their choice or of their forefathers. It has fallen to the Finns to inherit vast forests in the north. These forests are the fruits of the land in the same way olives, apples or grapes. Being an urban white-collar worker, I personally have the impression that the Finns, be they owners of much, little or no forest at all, wish to look upon and tend their forests with the care they would bestow on their back gardens.

Lasse Lehtinen